I0752690

# *Historic Restaurants* OF TUCSON

RITA CONNELLY

Published by American Palate
A Division of The History Press
Charleston, SC
www.historypress.net



*Front cover, top left*: author photo; *top right*: author photo; *bottom left*: courtesy Richard and Shana Oseran, Hotel Congress; *bottom right*: author photo.
*Back cover*: author photo; *inset*: courtesy Agro Land & Cattle Company.

First published 2018

ISBN 978-1-5402-2818-5

Library of Congress Control Number: 2017958377

*To the owners, chefs, kitchen staffs and front-of-the-house teams at all the fabulous restaurants in Tucson, who keep the magic going.*

*To my husband and family, for supporting my passion.*

# Contents

# Acknowledgements

To all the great people at The History Press, especially my acquisitions editor, Laurie Krill.

To Karyn Zoldan, friend and editor, for keeping this book tight.

Greg Casadei from the original Mama Louisa's.

Michael and Suzanne Elefante from Mama Louisa's, for all the info and photos and for answering my unending questions.

Sal Zagona Sr., Sal Zagona Jr. and Ande Motzkin from Caruso's, for the stories, the company and the ravioli.

Rebecca Ramey and Janet Seidler from the Blue Willow, live and on the phone.

Dr. Jonathan Mabry, City of Tucson Historic Preservation Officer, Planning and Development Services, for his help making sure I got things right and for help with images.

Carlotta Flores, for her stories of her great Tia Monica and El Charro Café.

Gerald Gay, for his intrepid detective work, photos and connections.

Dr. Theresa Levy, my Italian teacher and friend, for her translation help.

A.J. Flick, for her keen eye.

Kelli and Will Phillips, for the beautiful photos of and information about her grandparents, Gus and Kay Balon.

Scott Barker, for his rapid response.

Clyde Buzzard, for the photos and history from Lucky Wishbone and Mark Morris, the next generation of Lucky Wishbone.

Dale Calvert, Sherry Baran, Jim Campbell, Kade Mislinski and Dave Musso from Saguaro Corners.

Gina Yturralde from Pat's Drive In.

Teresa Shaar from El Minuto.

Yahtin and Naval Parekh from New Delhi Palace, for the lesson on Indian food and for your fabulous food.

Gordon Berger of Le Rendez-vous.

Susan Frank, for her numerous connections.

Dom Scala and Ed Irving, for all those eegee's insights.

Boyd Bartke from Robert's.

Aracely Gonzalez from Crossroads, for the shared information and her delicious dish.

Suzana Davila from Café Poca Cosa.

Jonathan Landeen from Jonathan's Cork.

Dave Hoffman and Connie Gilbert from Li'l Abner's.

Jimmy Lopez and the folks at "my little nest," Mi Nidito.

Dan Bates and Casey Wills from Pinnacle Peak, for their time and the beautiful menus.

Shana and Richard Oseran, for taking time from their vacation to talk about the Cup.

The Arizona Inn, for the photos.

Darryl Wong of Lotus Garden.

Michael Suarez, for the Lucky Wishbone clothing.

My Facebook friends, who, whenever I asked for their memories of certain restaurants, answered my pleas. (That's you, Marguerite Brown.)

My foodie friends Edie Jarolim, Norma Gentry, Matt Russell, Andi Berlin and Adam Lehrman, for their support and suggestions and the sharing of numerous dishes and drinks.

# Introduction

*Historic Restaurants of Tucson* is a collection of stories about the many establishments that have served the cravings of Tucson diners through the years.

When I told people that I was going to be writing a book about restaurants that have survived the trials and tribulations of the restaurant business in Tucson, invariably the reaction was, "Wow, how many of them can still be in business?" I don't have the exact number, but surprisingly, there are quite a few still going strong.

In deciding on which eateries to include, I had to ask myself, "Just what is a 'historic' restaurant?" Longevity played a part, but I also considered which restaurants made an impact on Tucson dining or on people's lives. Did the restaurant change the way people ate? Did it add to the culinary scene? What do people remember about a certain restaurant or a special meal? Are these restaurants part of the big picture?

I enlisted the help of friends, especially those who have lived in Tucson all their lives. I interviewed restaurateurs and chefs. Other restaurants are just some of my favorites or the ones that played a significant role in my life.

Deciding which diners or cafés to include proved frustrating. There are so many long-standing diners, all of which have their own following. Frank's/Francisco's (established in 1972) are two restaurants in one. Depending on the time of day, the place is either a full-blown diner or a cozy, neighborhood Mexican eatery. Bobo's (1978) boasts larger-than-your-plate pancakes and a waiting list any day of the week. At the Hungry Fox (1964), three-yolk

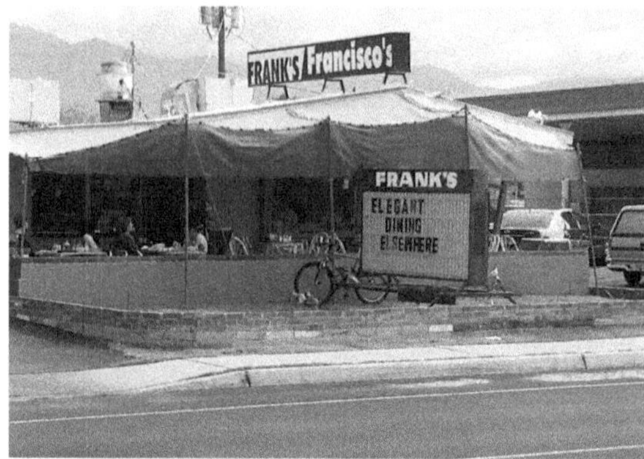


*Left*: Frank's/Francisco's is two restaurants in one. *Author photo.*

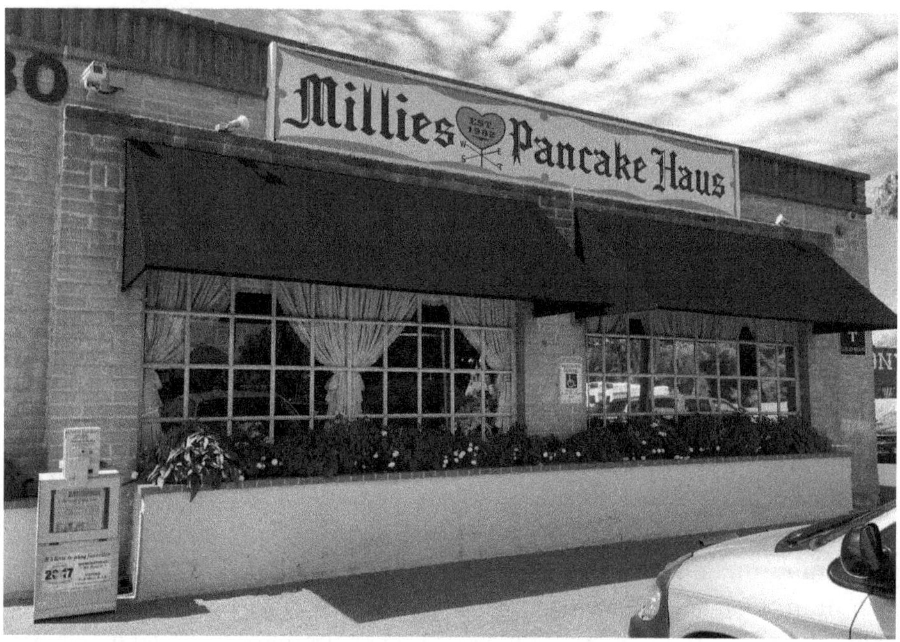


*Below*: Millie's Pancake Haus, for that international treat. *Author photo.*

omelets are the norm. Millie's Pancake Haus (1964) has international dishes like Russian blintzes, French omelets and Belgian waffles.

Still, there are so many not all could be included in this book. I apologize to those places and to readers who may not find their favorites.

In some ways, this book will be a companion piece to my first publication from The History Press, *Lost Restaurants of Tucson*. But you don't have to have read the first book to enjoy this one. *Historic Restaurants of Tucson* will give readers a detailed view of the history of dining in Tucson. I think it may make people hungry, too.

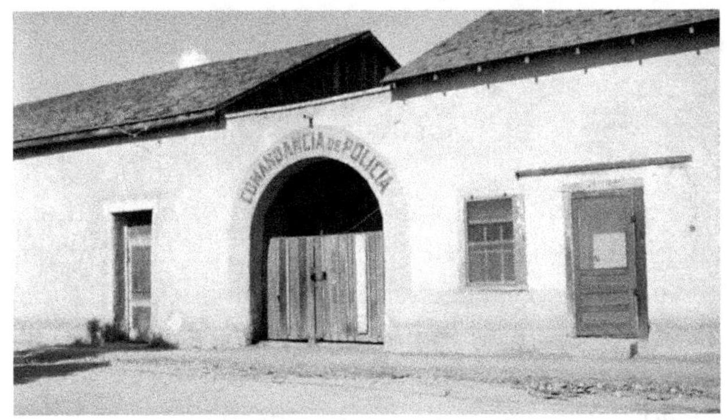


An early jail south of downtown. *Library of Congress.*

I've arranged the chapters in chronological order, because doing so was the best way to show how Tucson grew from a sleepy small town to the sparkling, vibrant desert city it is today. The book will also try to capture what was happening in the city and the world during each decade. It must be noted that the short introductions to each decade are not meant to be a definitive history of the times.

Research took me to restaurants all over town, to the Pima County Public Library and to the Arizona Historical Museum. I have tried to cite all sources—one book being *Tucson: The Life and Times of an American City* by C.L. Sonnichsen—but some of the stories have been such a big part of Tucson's history that they've been told over and over again, to the point that their origins have been lost. Some of the research involved amateur detective work; I would find a name or date online and then track people down with the stealth of Sherlock Holmes.

Most of the information came from the people involved: the owners, their relatives, friends who knew somebody who knew somebody. And I read plenty of obituaries. That could've been sad work but, instead, proved a motivator to tell the stories of these hardworking, passionate people.

The restaurants featured herein begin as far back as 1922; 1997 is the end of the historic timeline. If that latter date seems too recent, readers must remember that twenty years in the hospitality business is something to be admired. Studies have shown that 60 percent of restaurants fail in their first year; after five years, 80 percent of restaurants are shuttered. The fact that the restaurants mentioned in this book are thriving is a testament to the passion the owners have for their craft, and this book will celebrate those people and places. While I was writing, two restaurants I wanted to include closed. Midtown Molina's had been open for sixty-plus years; Delectables closed after forty years.

That end date also meant that several restaurants couldn't be included. Feast, which introduced Tucsonans to "tasteful takeout," and Wildflower, the first of renowned restaurateur Sam Fox's empire, were only two of several places that opened after 1997.

These are family stories, generational stories and stories of immigrants coming to America with hopes and dreams of a better life. They are success stories—restaurants were passed from one generation to the next, and then the next (and, in some cases, the next). Sadly, there just wasn't room for all the wonderful stories—the copper pot at Caruso's, the kitchen sink at Mama Louisa's and the night a bulldozer crashed into Lucky Wishbone.

Of course, several generations of owners also mean several generations of diners. As I talked with the owners and chefs from some of the oldest restaurants, they mentioned how common it is to have the people who ate at their restaurants years ago return with their children and grandchildren and how, as a result, long-term relationships have been built.

Other profiles in this book are more modern tales. Two college students turn a great idea into an empire. A young chef gets the chance to prove himself. A seafood restaurant in the desert finds success.

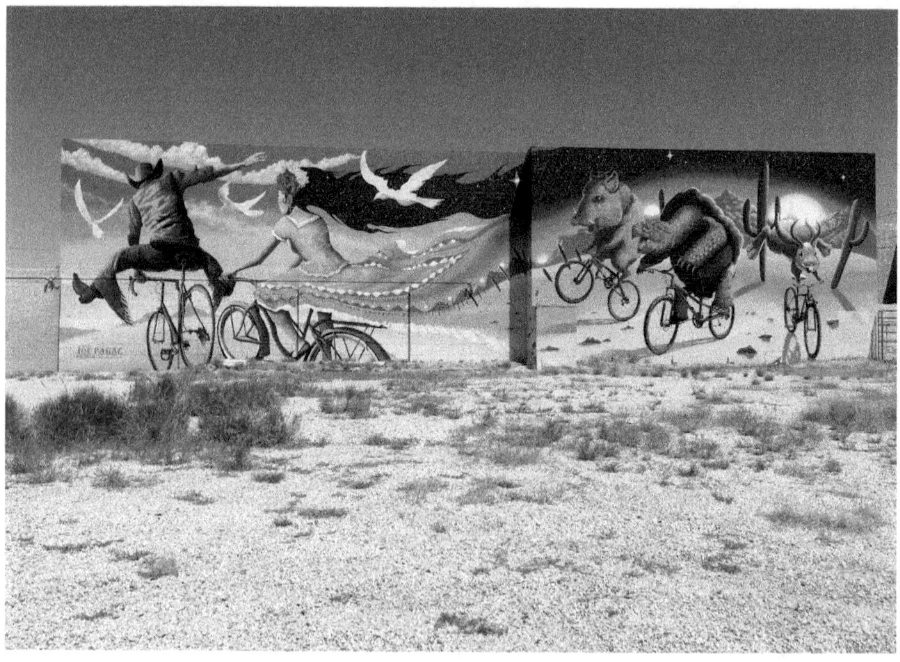

A mural from the City of Tucson Mural Project. Artist, Joe Pagac. *Author photo.*

Not all of these restaurants have had the same owners throughout their existence. I've included these establishments, because so many of them remain successful.

Readers will find stories of the many flavors of Tucson, flavors that go beyond what most people consider Tucson dining options. Granted, we Tucsonans believe we have the best Mexican food in America, and steakhouses seem to have lengthy histories. But the profiles in this book show that diners looking for Italian, Asian, American, French, southern and many other cuisines can satisfy their cravings at well-established restaurants.

From high-end dining to tiny sandwich shops; from mom-and-pop Mexican joints to classic cafés and diners; from hip eateries to hole-in-the-wall spots—this book will cover the best of decades of Tucson dining.

## FLAVORS FROM SOUTH OF THE BORDER

Most of southern Arizona was part of Sonora, Mexico, from 1822 until 1848, and these roots still play a huge role in the flavors of Tucson. The majority of the Mexican restaurants found in Tucson serve Sonoran-style food, and many non-Mexican restaurants utilize the same ingredients. And while restaurants come and go, diners have plenty of long-standing places to choose from when they're looking for authentic Sonoran dishes. Many of those restaurants are located in South Tucson.

South Tucson is a city unto itself. One square mile in size, this tiny burg is completely surrounded by Tucson. The city lines blur a little, but South Tucson has a look and feel of its own, thanks in part to the many restaurants that can be found there. Most have been in operation for thirty, forty and even fifty years. South Tucson restaurants could almost be the subject of a separate book.

In December 2015, Tucson was named a "City of Gastronomy" by the United Nations Educational, Scientific and Cultural Organization (UNESCO) as part of its Creative Cities Network. Tucsonans take pride in this prestigious designation, especially since it was the first U.S. city to have the title. (San Antonio was named a City of Gastronomy in 2017.) This City of Gastronomy theme is woven throughout the book.

Another central theme is the sense of community, which is apparent throughout the city and in the hospitality industry. The connections in Tucson's culinary community are, in some ways, complicated and convoluted.

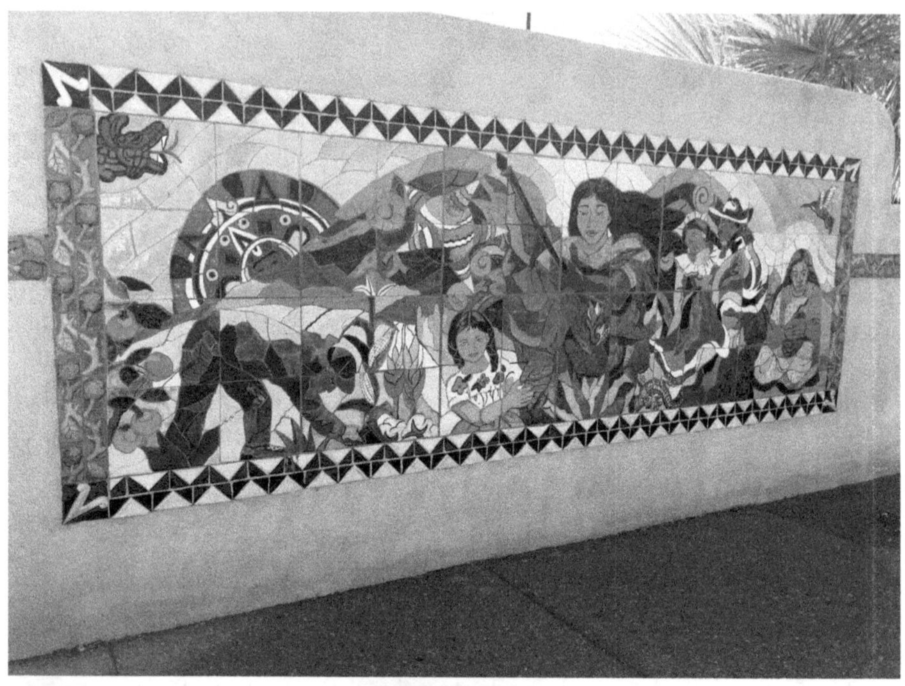

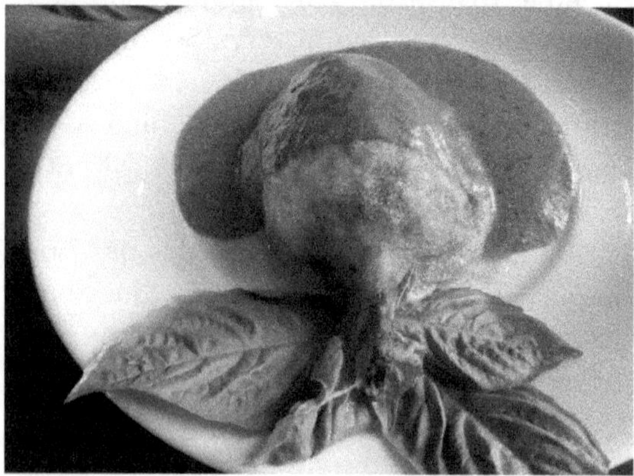

*Above:* A mosaic on South Fourth Avenue. *Author photo.*

*Left*: Chile relleno. *Author photo.*

Nevertheless, they are strong and were instrumental in the success of many restaurants found here.

Special sections of the book include relevant information about the people, places and entities that play important roles in Tucson gastronomy.

I have tried to paint a well-balanced picture of Tucson's rich culinary history.

# TUCSON'S DIVERSE FOOD STORY REACHES AN INTERNATIONAL AUDIENCE

In December 2015, Tucson earned the City of Gastronomy designation from UNESCO as part of its Creative Cities Network. That Tucson earned the designation was enough of a reason to boast. But even more impressive is the fact that Tucson is one of only twenty-eight in the world to be awarded this title. This put Tucsonans in a rarified group—other cities sharing the title include Parma, Italy; Ensenada, Mexico; and Phuket, Thailand.

Members of the national and international press were surprised that UNESCO gave the designation to an out-of-the-mainstream desert city. After all, what grows in the desert? But a passionate group of people knew better. In 2014, Dr. Gary Nabhan, professor in the University of Arizona's Southwest Center, approached Mayor Jonathan Rothschild about partnering on the application. They invited other important entities in the local food system to help flesh out the application. The core group consisted of the University of Arizona, the Santa Cruz Valley Heritage Alliance, *Edible Baja Arizona* (the local edition of the *Edible* magazine group), the mayor and Dr. Jonathan Mabry, the city's historic preservation officer and city archaeologist.

The first application was denied, but UNESCO indicated that Tucson was well qualified and encouraged the city to try again. Mabry led the group effort to rewrite the application, which had been completely revamped, with different questions and a new format. Through an announcement on the Creative Cities Network website, the application task force learned that their two-year effort was successful.

In an article in the November/December 2015 edition of *Edible Baja Arizona*, Dr. Mabry said, "This designation puts Tucson and its southern Arizona food shed on the global map as the capital of Southwestern borderlands cuisine and a center of food system innovation."

The city's application highlighted the following points:

> *From the desk of Dr. Jonathan Mabry:*
> * *The city's long agricultural history. During a series of projects to clear the path for expansion of I-10 and new development west of downtown, archaeologists discovered evidence of agricultural life dating back more than four thousand years. (The proof came when corn they found was radiocarbon-dated.) Mission Garden demonstrates Tucson's four-thousand-plus-year, culturally layered agricultural history at the historical location of*

*a Spanish Colonial period garden that supported the San Agustin Mission that served the O'Odham natives of Tucson's birthplace.*

* *The largest number of foods listed on the Slow Food Ark of Taste grown within one hundred miles, more than any other city in North America.*

* *A culturally diverse cuisine. Native American, Mexican, Mission-style Mediterranean and American-style Ranch Cowboy cuisines now blend with food traditions introduced by more recent immigrants.*

* *2015 initiatives by the City of Tucson to create a food policy council and a revision of urban agricultural regulations so that locals can grow, create and sell their products.*

* *A growing commitment to addressing food insecurity. Numerous programs developed by the University of Arizona, Pima County and the Southern Arizona Community Food Bank teach healthy food practices, offer instructions on planting home gardens and establish regulations and best practices for starting food-related businesses.*

* *Innovative approaches to conserving and disseminating desert-adapted seeds. Native Seeds/SEARCH, a local nonprofit cofounded by Nabhan,*

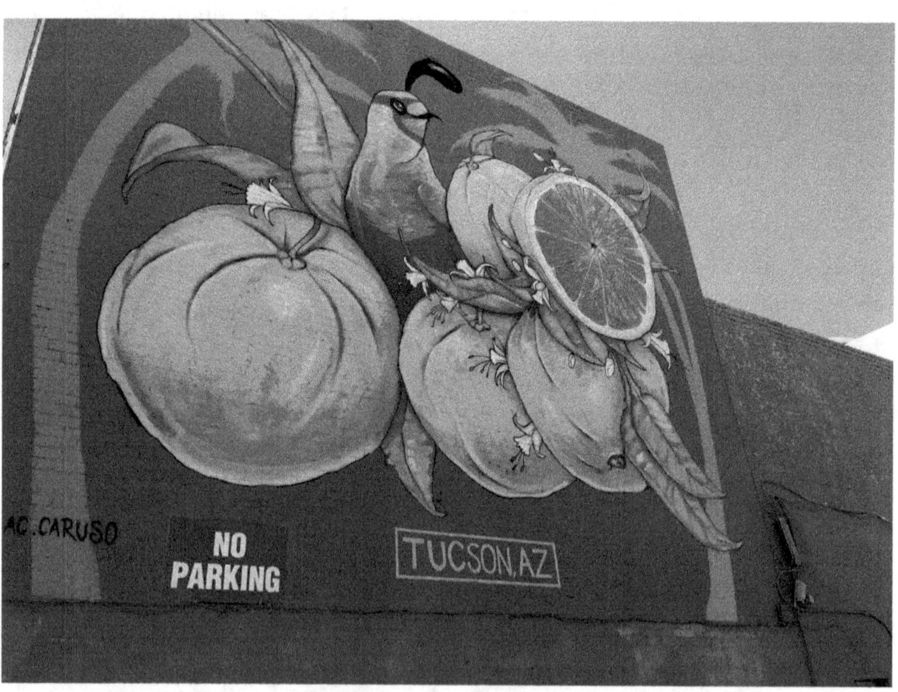


This foodie mural is part of the City of Tucson Mural Project. Artist, Isaac Caruso. *Author photo.*

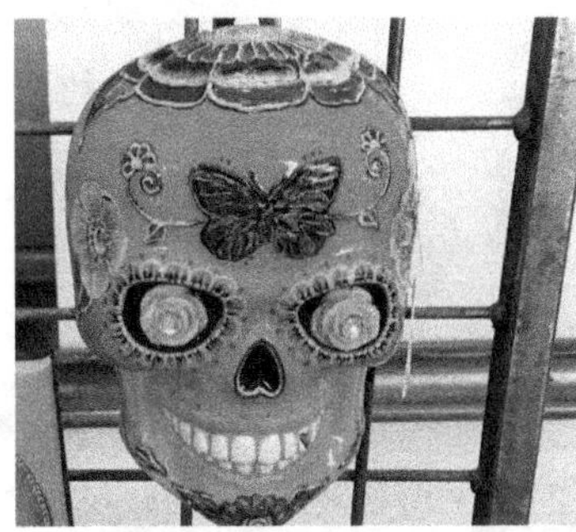

Day of the Dead mask. *Author photo.*

*is dedicated to the conservation, sharing and education of desert borderlands heritage seeds and crops. The Pima County Public Library system distributes free desert-adapted seeds through its Seed Library program.*

** Creation of a new Center for Regional Food Studies and a food studies program at the University of Arizona.*

** The rising number of farmers markets, artisanal food and beverage producers and food festivals. One such festival, Tucson Meet Yourself, has been celebrating the numerous ethnic foods and cultures that can be found here for more than forty years.*

** Creative chefs are using the ancient foods of the desert in new and delicious ways. Buds from the cholla cactus, tepary beans and mesquite pods are showing up on menus all over the city.*

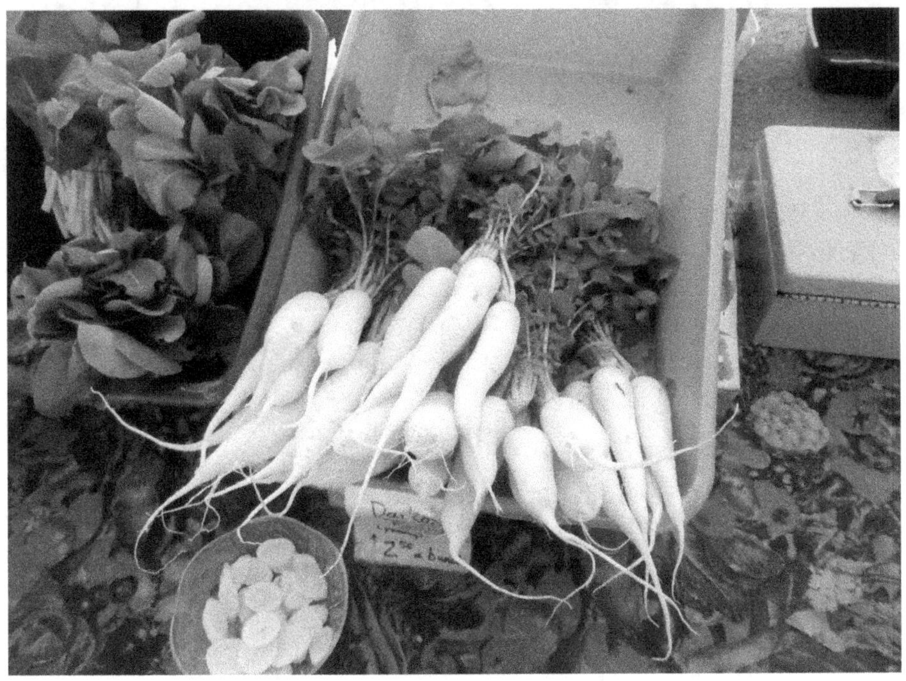

Fresh vegetables from one of the many farmers' markets. *Author photo.*

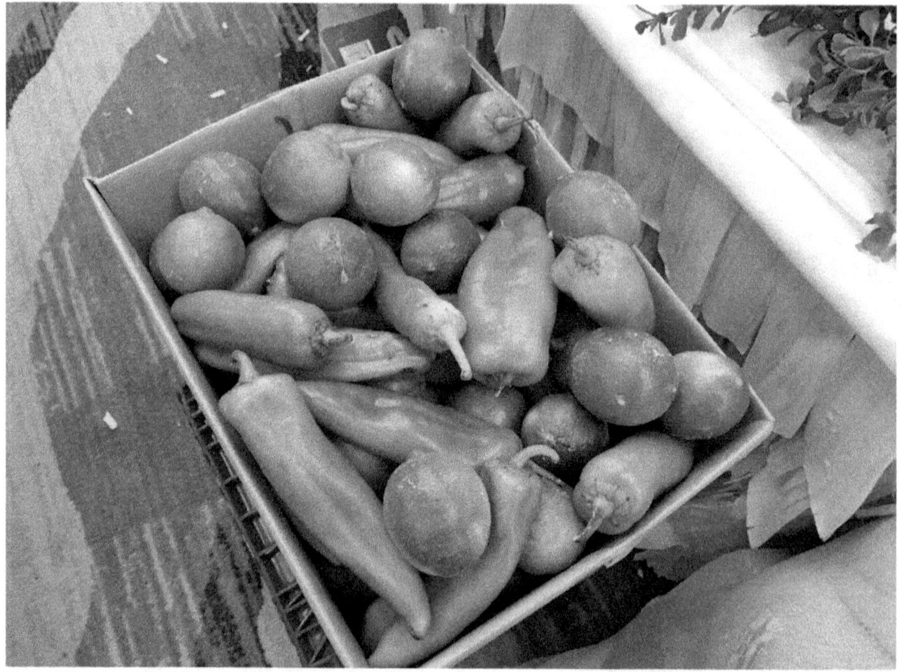

This box of green chiles promises great food to come. *Author photo.*

The designation requires periodic reports of what Tucson is doing to leverage its UNESCO status to support the local food economy, address issues in its food system and share knowledge with other cities in the Creative Cities Network. The first year's report demonstrated the area's continuing efforts to enhance Tucson's culture of gastronomy.

If the past is any indication of Tucson's culinary future, things are looking bright and promising.

# 1

# From Saloons to Fine Dining

## A Brief History of the Culinary and Cultural Scene in Tucson

Tucson has long been a foodie place, even as far back as the 1870s, when George Hand, a Civil War hero who settled in territorial Tucson, wrote about his dining adventures in his diary. Most of his meals were at one or another of the many saloons found in early Tucson.

Located in Pima County, Tucson is Arizona's second-largest city. Tucson's location made it a prime destination for settlers, including native tribes, as far back as four thousand years ago. It is one of America's oldest settlements. The location was an ideal stopping point for travelers heading to California from New Orleans or for people going to Mexico.

The sun shines 310 days a year, and the average temperatures are eighty-three degrees (high) and fifty-eight degrees (low). Mountains surround the city and allow for plenty of outdoor activities year-round. Of course, there is the Sonoran Desert. Newcomers are surprised at how lush the desert is and awed by its beauty. The Sonoran Desert is the only place where saguaro cactus—those spiny, multi-armed giants seen in cowboy movies—grow.

Architecture is a blend of old and new. Tucson is home to the Arizona Ballet Company, the Tucson Symphony, the Arizona Opera Company and hundreds of arts groups, galleries and museums. These factors have created a place rich in culture and natural beauty.

What follows is a timeline of Tucson's history, with an emphasis on cuisine and culture.

Circa 2000 BC

The first traces of farming in the area date back some four thousand years. The Santa Cruz River, which flowed freely until the 1890s, was a source of water. An archaeological dig discovered that the early people also developed a series of irrigation canals.

1692 Father Kino brings cattle and wheat when he establishes a mission in Primera Alta. The introduction of both items changed the diet of the native peoples in southern Arizona.

1775 Presidio de Tucson is established by Colonel Hugo O'Conor in the name of Spain.

1853 Gadsden Purchase is enacted, and the Arizona Territory becomes part of the United States. Tucson would live under five flags: American, Spanish, Mexican, the State of Arizona and, for a short time in 1862, the Confederacy.

1865 Camp Lowell is established seven miles east of Tucson to provide protection from the Apaches. In 1879, the name is changed to Fort Lowell.

1866 Alex Levin opens a beer garden that would become the center of Tucson entertainment for decades.

1870s The Wong family arrives and opens the O.K. Restaurant on the corner of Church Plaza and Mesilla Street. As more Chinese moved to Tucson, they created truck farms by leasing land from

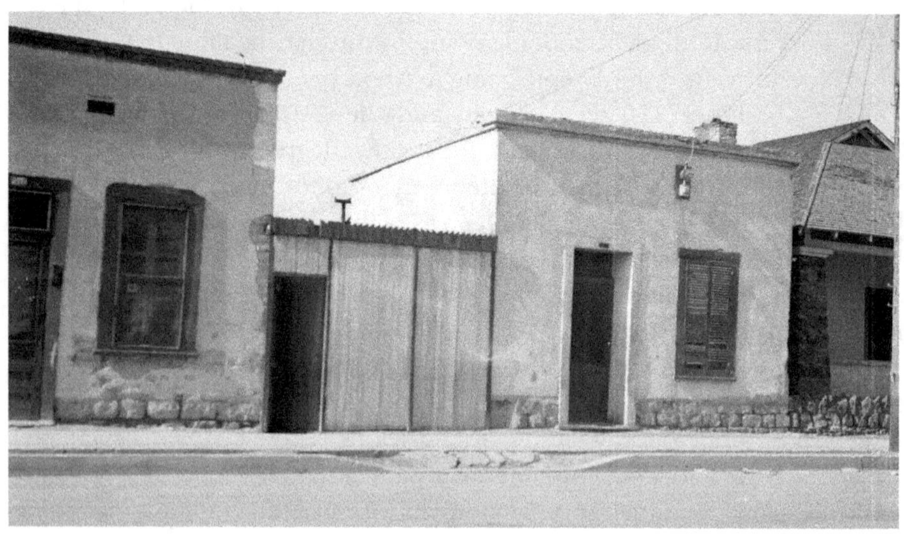

Court Street. *Library of Congress.*

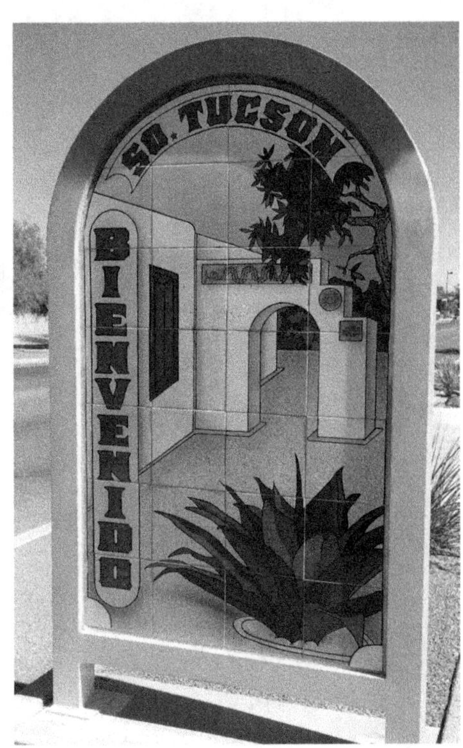


*Right*: Mosaics are plentiful on South Fourth Avenue. *Author photo*.

*Below*: Padre Kino brought beef and wheat to the Sonoran Desert. *Author photo*.

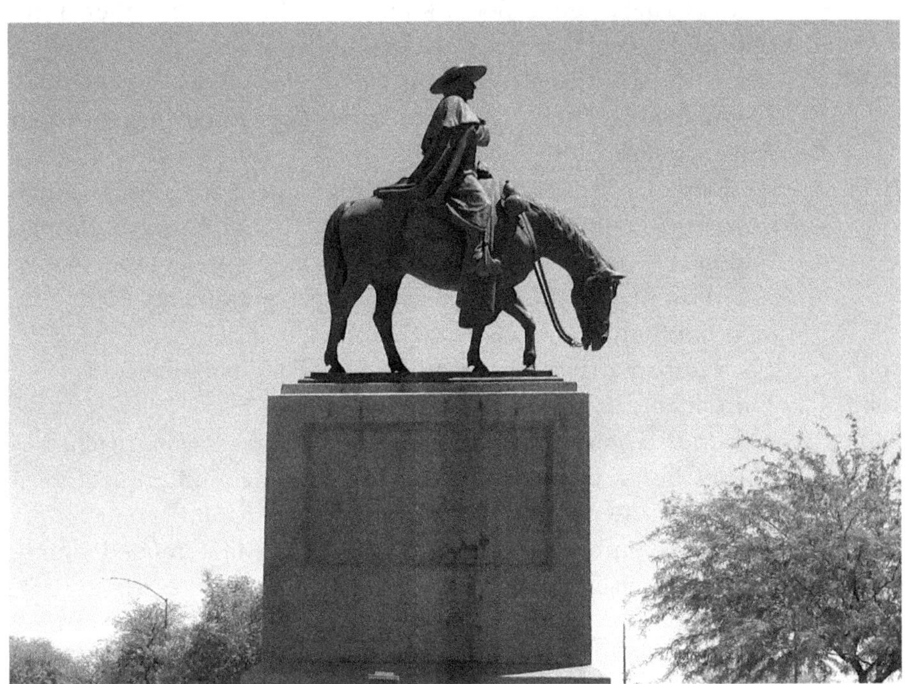

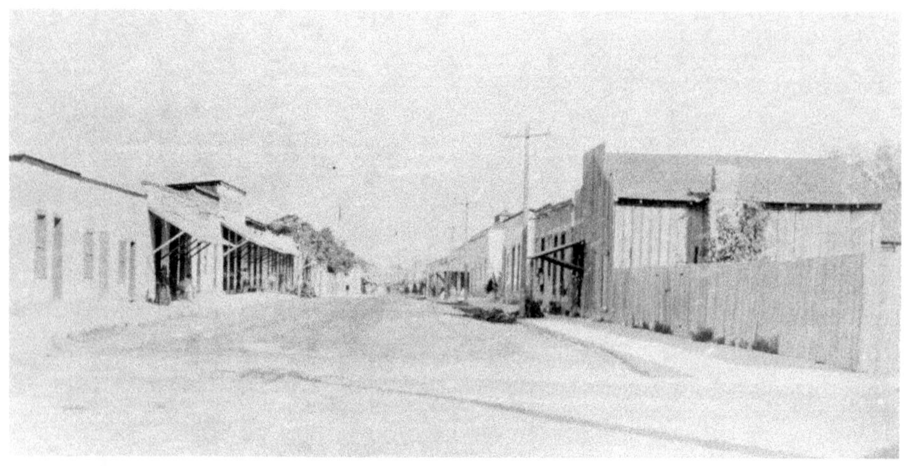

An early view of downtown. *Library of Congress.*

Mexican owners. They grew fresh vegetables ranging from strawberries to bitter melon and sold the produce to both homes and businesses. The concept of *guanxi*, a bonding with families for support and protection, became a kith relationship with the Mexican population. Many opened grocery stores that were central to the neighborhoods for decades. In the 1960s, there were eighty Chinese groceries in the downtown area.

1870 The *Arizona Citizen*, Tucson's first daily newspaper, is published. The name was later changed to *Tucson Citizen*. The paper ceased publication in 2009.

1874 President Ulysses S. Grant establishes the San Xavier Indian Reservation on the land occupied by the Tohono O'odham Indian Nation. The Pasqua Pueblo Yaqui Nation, the area's other Native American people, did not receive full recognition until 1978.

1877 Incorporation of the town of Tucson.

1880 The railroad arrives, changing the way Tucsonans live and eat.

1883 The City of Tucson is chartered.

1885 A court decision (*W.A. Dalton et al. v. Leo Carrillo et al.*) is reached in which Chinese truck farmers win the right to continue use of local sources to water their crops.

1890 Rossi's Columbia Restaurant, one of the first refined dining establishments in the heart of the city, opens.

1891 The University of Arizona is founded. City fathers had wanted Tucson to be the capital, but thanks to bad weather and political

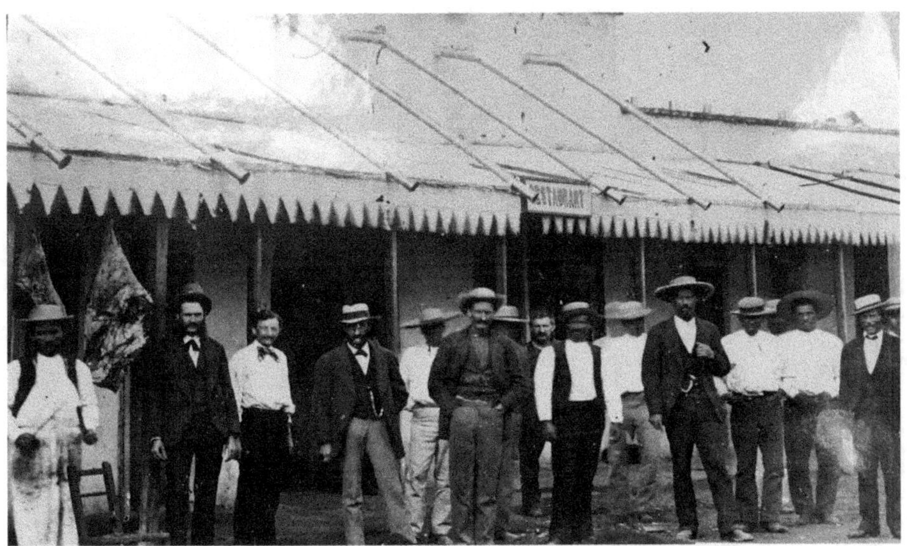

A group of unidentified men in front of a butcher shop. *From the collection of the Tucson Museum of Art & Historic Block.*

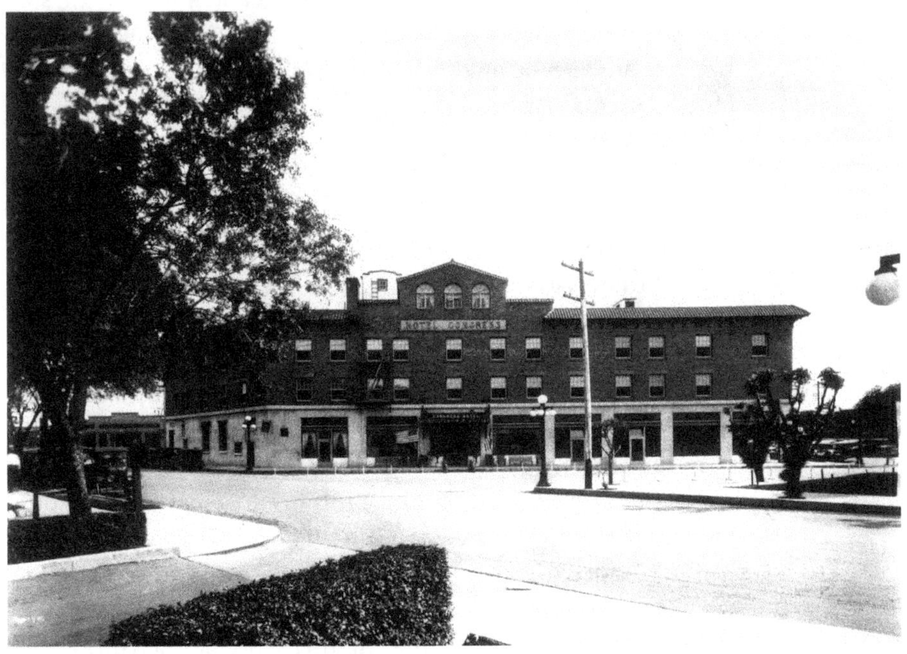


Downtown Tucson doesn't look the same, but Hotel Congress endures. *Courtesy Richard and Shana Oseran, Hotel Congress.*

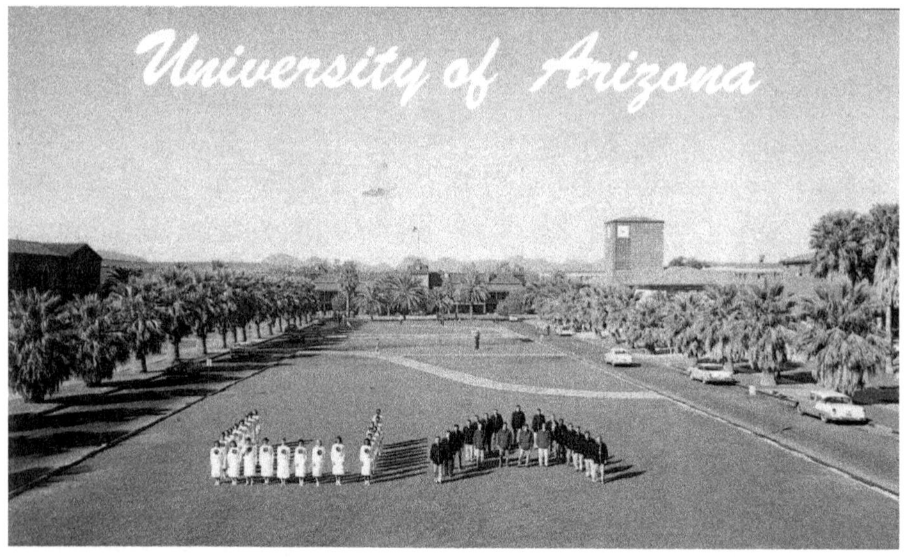


The University of Arizona Mall. *From the collection of the author.*

finagling, the title went to Prescott. State leaders tossed Tucson a bone by giving the city the university. While at the time the gesture was not appreciated, in the long run, having the university benefited Tucson and brought world influences and flavors here.

1893 The first library opens.

1899 Tucson's first automobile hits the streets.

1910 The first airplane arrives.

1912 Arizona becomes a state.

1918 Congress Street is paved.

1920 University of Arizona enrollment surpasses one thousand students.

1922 The Tucson Sunshine Climate Club is formed with the specific goal of promoting Tucson tourism across the United States.

1924 The Tucson City Directory lists thirty-five restaurants in Tucson.

1927 Charles Lindbergh dedicates Davis-Monthan Field, the nation's largest municipal airfield.

1928 El Conquistador Hotel on Broadway opens to accommodate the influx of new tourists.

1929 The Pioneer Hotel, Tucson's first high-rise hotel, opens. Built by successful merchant Henry Steinfeld, the hotel became the center of high society's activity.

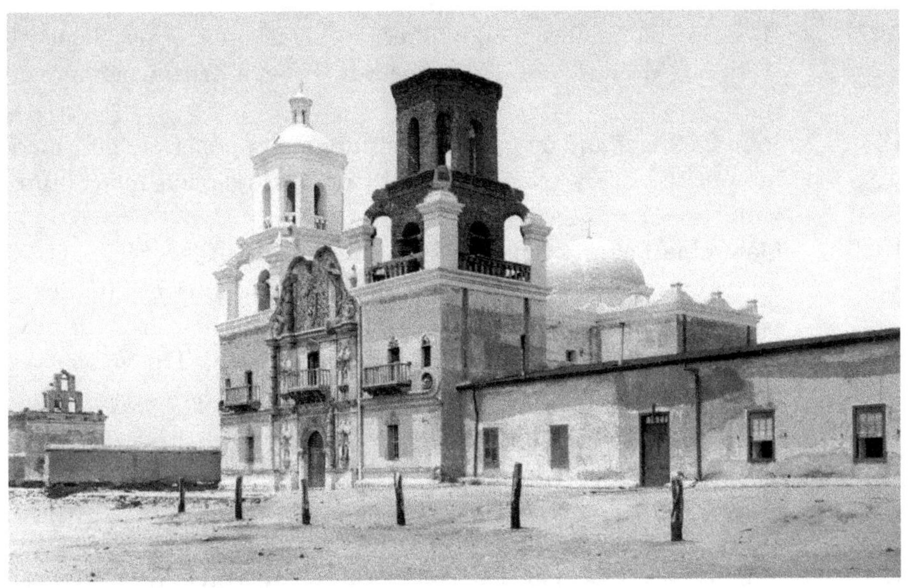

The White Dove of the Desert, San Xavier del Bac, located on the Tohono O'odham Indian Reservation. *Library of Congress.*

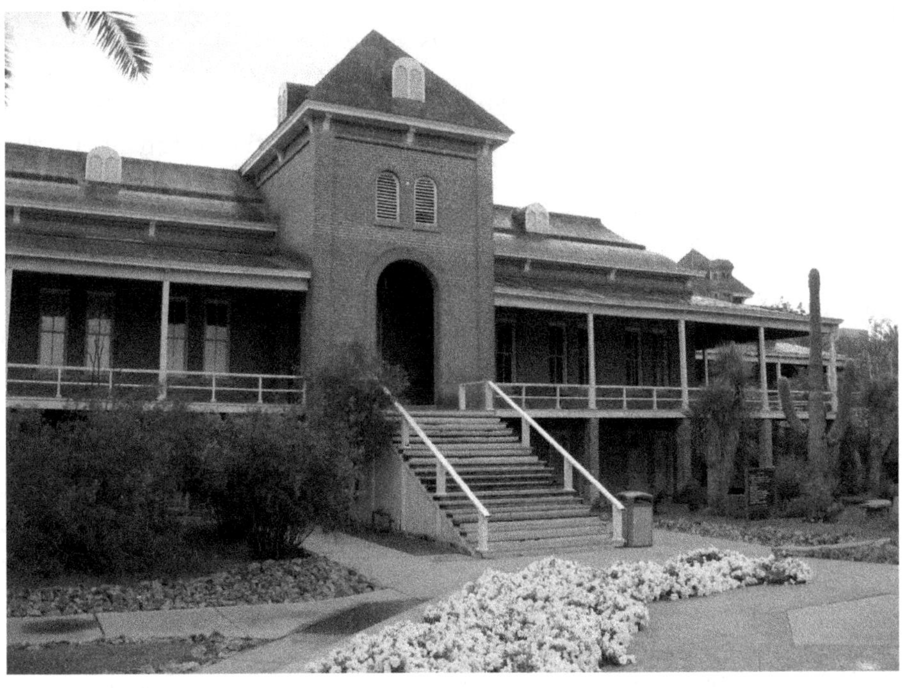

Old Main was the first building on the University of Arizona campus. *Wikimedia Commons, Ken Lund.*

1933 By a proclamation signed by President Herbert Hoover, Saguaro National Monument is established. In 1994, it became a national park.

1934 John Dillinger and his gang are captured after police are informed by tourists. Every year, the Hotel Congress reenacts the capture with two days of festivities.

1939 Columbia Pictures builds a set for the movie *Arizona*, which kicks off a long relationship between Hollywood and Tucson. Hundreds of movies and television shows were shot in and around the city, and movie stars dined at restaurants in town. The movie set became Old Tucson, a major tourist attraction to this day.

1940 South Tucson incorporates as a city.

1941 An army air base, Tucson Army Air Field, is established on the site of the municipal airport, which, six months later, was renamed Davis-Monthan Field.

1945 The Boneyard, near Davis-Monthan Air Force Base, opens. Here, due to Tucson's perfect climate, old planes are kept for posterity.

1947 Major League Baseball spring training begins in Tucson. The Cleveland Indians were the first of many over a sixty-year period to practice there. The last teams, the Arizona Diamondbacks and the Colorado Rockies, moved to the Phoenix area in 2011.

1951 Hughes Missiles Systems opens a plant in Tucson, creating well-paying jobs and an influx of new people moving to the city.

1953 The first television station in Tucson, KOPO, begins broadcasting. Call letters were later changed to KOLD.

1956 Elvis Presley has a concert at the Rodeo Grounds. Tucson "arrived" on the rock 'n' roll scene.

1960–61 El Con Mall opens across from the city's largest park, then known as Randolph Park. Modern buildings and a wide assortment of stores signaled a move away from downtown as the center of activity.

1961 The first McDonald's in Tucson is franchised.

**Carry-Out Cafe Planned**

Mrs. Loraine Harsh, a resident of Tucson since 1957, has obtained the local franchise for McDonald's Carry-out Restaurant chain and will open the first local unit in a new special building at 5351 E. Speedway Sept. 19.

Ray Kroc, president of the chain, which now has 290 units throughout the country, visited Tucson and surveyed its possibilities before granting the franchise. The site was leased through Dick Hall Realty. Investment in building and equipment will total about $125,000.

McDonald's restaurants are strictly carry-out, with menus limited to sandwiches, soft drinks, milk, coffee and French fries appealing especially to youth. The local unit will employ about 30 people, all male help.

Mrs. Harsh formerly owned and operated the Humbolt Realty in Chicago. Since coming to Tucson she has been in secretarial work.



McDonald's comes to Tucson, February 1961. Arizona Daily Star.

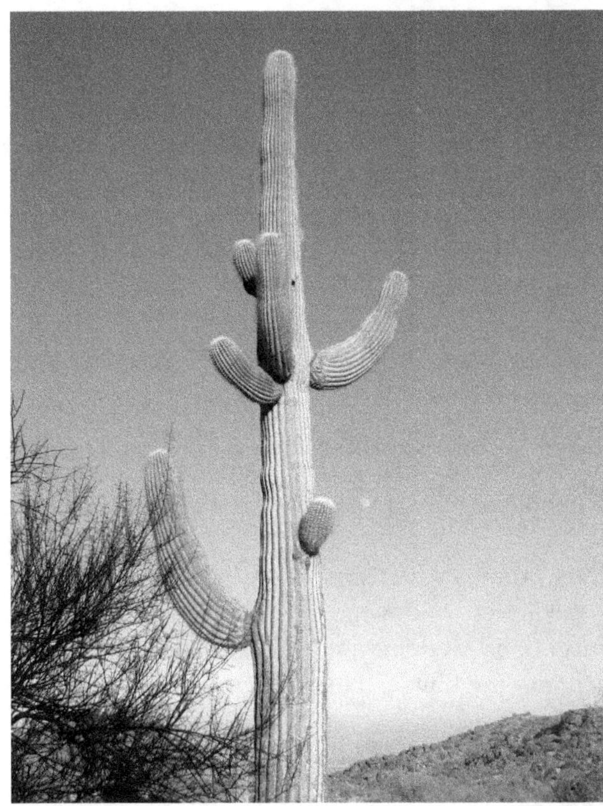

*Left*: The stately Saguaro cactus is a symbol of Arizona and only grows in the Sonoran Desert.

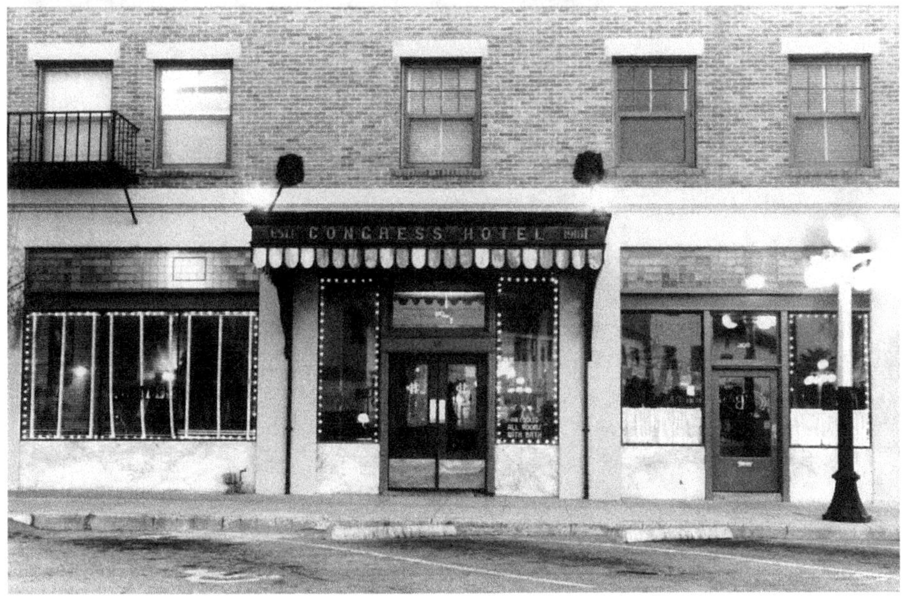


*Below*: The Congress Street entrance to Hotel Congress. *Courtesy Richard and Shana Oseran, Hotel Congress.*

1963 City of Tucson passes an ordinance outlawing the practice of not serving people due to race or ethnicity.

1967 With the vision of a modern city that would attract business and industry, Tucson begins intensive urban renewal projects. Monies were federally funded, and 263 buildings covering eighty acres were wiped out in the downtown area. Depending on one's point of view, this was either a fantastic step forward or the destruction of Hispanic, African American and Chinese lives and culture.

1969 Pima Community College opens its doors.

1970 *Life* magazine calls Speedway Boulevard "The Ugliest Street in America." Tucsonans disagree.

1970 The initial Fourth Avenue Street Fair is held. Starting out small, this twice-a-year festival of arts, crafts, music and food now attracts 600,000 people a year and is considered one of the city's premier events.

1970 The Pioneer Hotel, Tucson's first skyscraper, goes up in flames. The hotel was the jewel of downtown and the place people gathered for conventions, weddings, cocktails or lunch. Twenty-nine people, including the builder Henry Steinfeld and his wife,

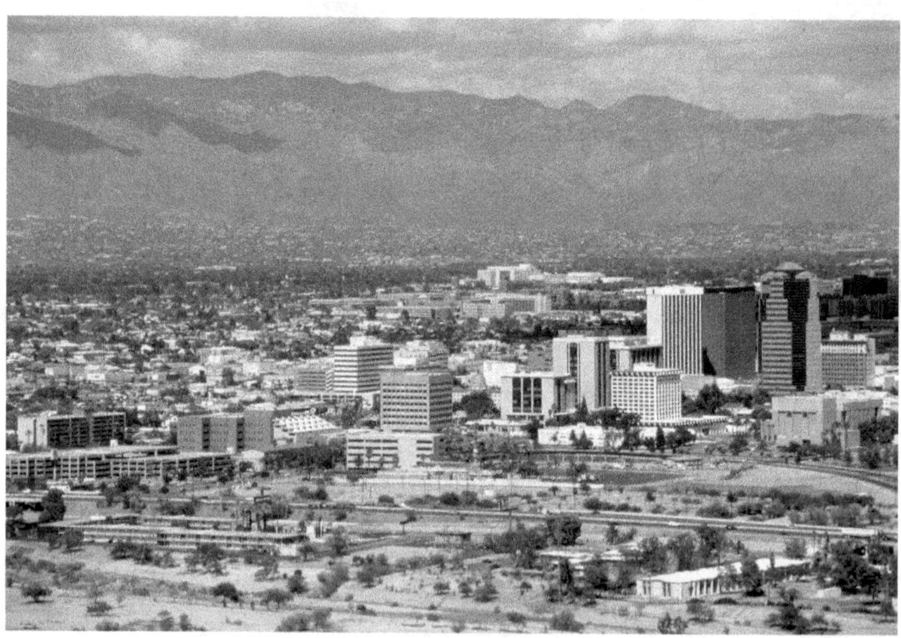

Modern city view from "A" Mountain. *Http://www.fhwa.dot.gov/byways/photos.*

died. The city subsequently changed building codes to ensure that such a tragedy never happened again.

1976 In an effort to make citizens aware of the need to conserve water in the hot summer months, the city creates "Beat the Peak" and its duck mascot, Pete the Beak.

1983 The University of Arizona hires basketball coach Lute Olsen. The hire ushers in a new era for UA athletics, making the basketball program one of the outstanding teams in the country. Olsen coached the team for twenty-five years and led the team to its only national championship in 1997.

1992 The Central Arizona Project begins. The canal was designed to deliver water from the Colorado River to southern Arizona. Results were a disaster. The mineral content differed from the groundwater Tucson had been using and released rust and corrosion into the water system, especially in older homes. Water was brown and smelly. The city had to pay more than $700,000 in damages and return many homes back to groundwater.

1998 Tucson Originals, a group of restaurateurs created to promote Tucson and support one another, is born.

2015 Tucson is designated a World City of Gastronomy by UNESCO.

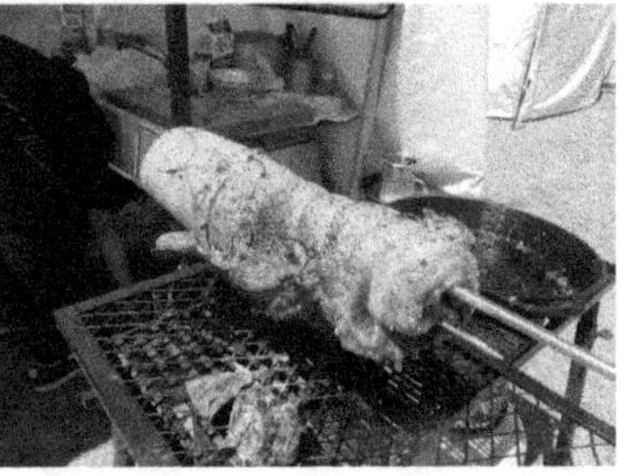

The beginnings of tacos el pastor at one of Tucson's many food festivals. *Author photo.*

2

# Early Eats

## 1920s–1930s

## 1920s

*Population: Tucson, 20,292; Pima County, 34,680*

Post–World War I Tucson escaped much of the turmoil the rest of America was experiencing, but daily life was still filled with tribulations and troubles. Prices on daily goods, such as gasoline and food, were soaring, due in part to greedy profiteers.

Federal government intervention was important, but on the local level, action had to be swift. The city began buying surplus government food and selling it at rock-bottom prices. A public market was established in St. Augustine Plaza, allowing a place for local farmers to sell their wares and housewives to buy them at reasonable prices, which relieved the stress of making ends meet for all involved.

Water was also at a premium. In 1920, the city enforced a strict moratorium on watering during the day.

In 1922, a group of businessmen created the Sunshine Climate Club, whose sole purpose was to promote tourism and perhaps attract new residents. Each member contributed $1,000. The monies were used for advertising in magazines and newspapers in the East and Midwest. In all ways, the Sunshine Climate Club succeeded, as visitors increased almost daily and many of them took up permanent residence in the Old Pueblo.

Restaurants were few and far between; the city directory listed a total of thirty-five in 1924. They ranged from fine dining in hotels to tiny tearooms for the ladies.

Overall, the 1920s were good to Tucson. After decades of being a sleepy, dusty cow town, Tucson was starting to look and feel like a city.

## EL CHARRO (1922)
### FROM AN INTERVIEW WITH CARLOTTA FLORES

The story of El Charro Café is that of two women who, although separated by a generation, shared a love of family and a passion for food. Together, they created a restaurant that is today America's oldest Mexican restaurant continually owned and operated by the same family, as well as a thriving culinary empire.

The restaurant is El Charro. Charros are Mexican horsemen, known for their colorful outfits and romantic charm. The women are founder Monica

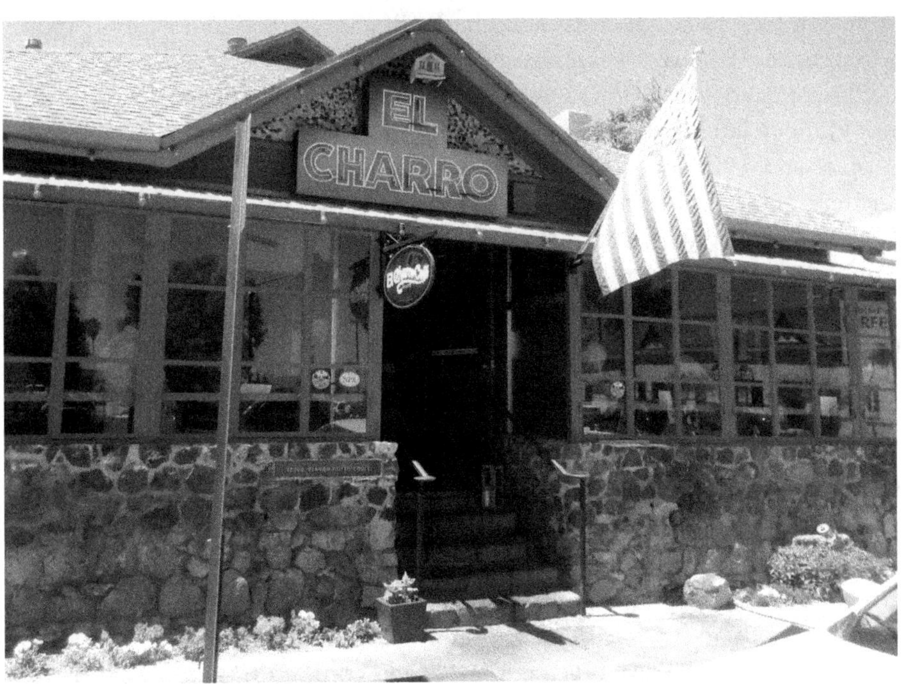


People wait for hours for a table at the El Charro on Court Street in downtown. *Author photo.*

Flin and her great-niece, Carlotta Flores. Born in 1887, Monica Flin wasn't your typical young Mexican woman. She didn't have children of her own. She liked to hunt. After getting married and divorced (romantically, four times to the same man), she lived alone. She spoke French, Spanish and English. And she opened a restaurant—El Charro—on her own in 1922.

Flin was the eldest of eight children of Jules Flin, a stonemason who had been commissioned by the local bishop to create the original St. Augustine Cathedral. Jules was from France. He married a local woman and built a small but sturdy home just north of downtown on Court Street using the basalt rock found on nearby Tumamoc Hill.

"She was a pistol," said Flores, who spent hours in Tia Monica's kitchen with her sisters and cousins. "She didn't believe that women had to be quiet."

Flores noted that Flin was part nana, part Auntie Mame. She was the aunt who took the whole crew on overnight train trips to Los Angeles to shop or who bought the toy the parents said no to or prepared wild game she herself caught and killed. "It's where I learned to eat rabbit and venison," Flores said. Even her card parties were interesting. During Prohibition, Flin held card parties at the restaurant. All the women would gather at a big round table and have "tea." If the teacup had a lime in it, the señora was drinking a margarita. If there was an olive, the tea was a martini.

Flin opened the original restaurant on Fourth Avenue at the site that would much later become Caruso's Italian Restaurant. Family lore tells how people would order food and then Flin would quickly run out to a nearby farmer's stand, get the necessary ingredients and return to the restaurant to cook and serve the meal. After the customers had paid for the food, Flin would then pay the farmer.

The second El Charro was on the other side of downtown, at what is now the Temple of Music and Art. Flin lived in the back, and her kitchen is where many of Flores's fondest memories of Tia Monica took place. "She was the best cook, but in a different way," said Flores.

A third move to Broadway was where El Charro—and Flin—became truly successful.

Food at the early El Charro wasn't all Mexican. No doubt, there were influences of her French heritage, but Flin took advantage of the nearby Greyhound Bus station and served American fare. On Thanksgiving, she prepared both an American turkey dinner and a Mexican turkey dinner for her customers, and she would send everyone home with their own turkey.

Thanks to the success of El Charro, Flin was able to travel. On one of her trips to Mexico City, she became awed by the beauty of Popucatepeti,

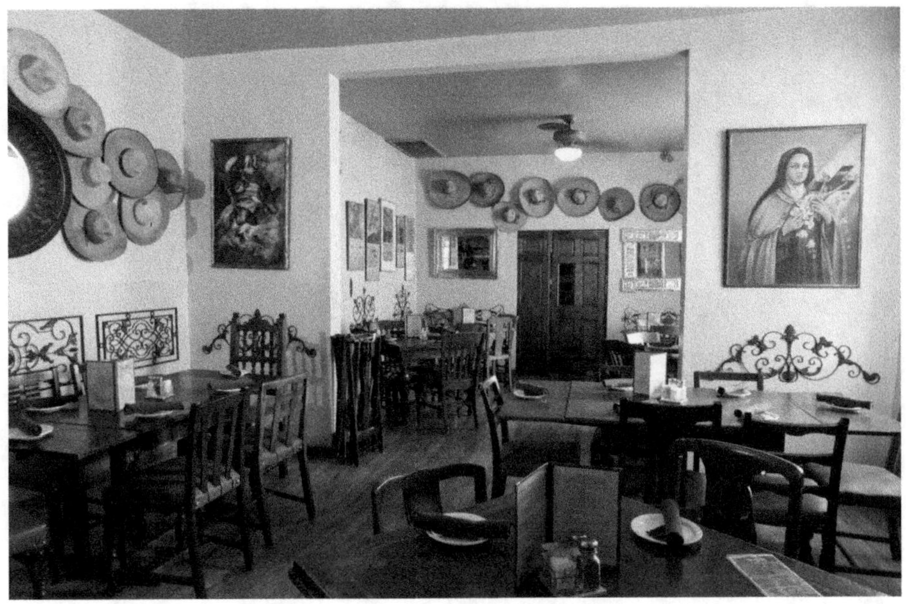

The walls of El Charro tell many stories. *Courtesy El Charro.*

the active volcano just outside the city. She came home and created a special salad that she named a *topopo* ("volcano" in Spanish). The salad has a corn tortilla base topped with refried beans and a conical pile of shredded lettuce trimmed with cheese, avocado and chicken or other meat. Topopos are a staple on local restaurant menus. Cheese crisps and deep-fried tacos dorado were her original creations, too.

Then there's perhaps the most famous Flin creation of all: the kitchen accident known as a chimichanga. While making burros (the term used in Arizona for burritos) for her nieces and nephews, Flin dropped one burro into a pot of hot oil. Flin was about to utter a Mexican swear word but caught herself and said "chimichanga," which loosely translates to "thingamajig."

Flin also popularized the seasoned, sun-dried beef called carne seca, which she dried in the back room of the restaurant. Today, the beef is dried in cages on the roof, and carne seca is one of the most popular items on the menu.

Around 1968, times got tough for Flin. Urban renewal was in full swing, and the neighborhoods around the restaurant were disappearing. She fell behind in her taxes, so she decided to move the restaurant to the family home on Court Street.

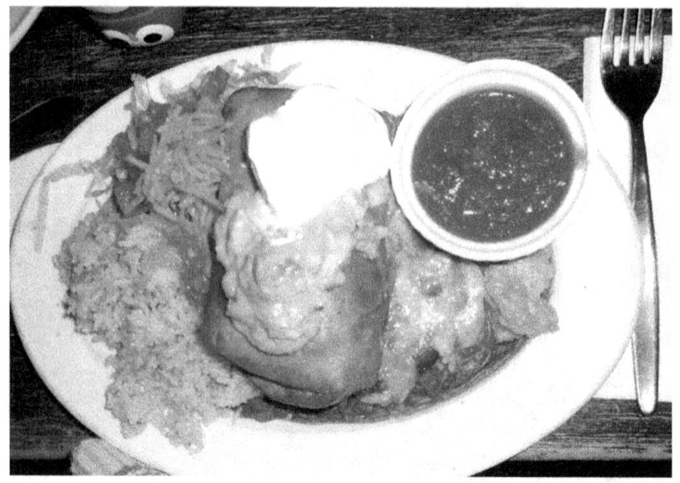

No matter what anyone tells you, the chimichanga was created in Tucson. *Author photo.*

Flin ran the restaurant until 1972 and handed her spatula over to her niece Zarina Dunn, Flores's mother. Dunn took care of the place for a little while, but then the word went out to the family that they were going to put the restaurant up for sale. Flores, her husband, Ray, and their two young sons were living in Los Angeles, and they came to town to help. "When I walked in this place," said Flores, "I said 'no.' We can't sell it." She was working in the food industry in California, so running the family restaurant was a logical step.

Under her guidance and with the help of her husband, sons Ray Jr. and Marcos and daughter Candace Flores Carrillo, El Charro grew into an empire. In addition to the three El Charros in Tucson, there is a more casual spot, Sir Veza's Taco Garage, and a commissary where "nanas still make all the food." Three Sir Veza's can be found in Phoenix, plus a restaurant at the MGM Hotel in Las Vegas called Hecho en Vegas. And for a taste of El Charro at home, there's Carlotta's Kitchen, a line of quality food products. An outpost, El Charro Under the Sea, is located in the submarine USS *Tucson*.

But it's the Court Street site that is the heart and soul of El Charro. The walls are filled with well-worn charro hats, serapes, posters of charros and their beautiful ladies and a mix of Mexican tchotchkes. Heavy wooden tables are tucked close together. Framed articles from *Gourmet*, *USA Today* and other national and local publications are also a part of the decor. One article Flores is especially proud of is from the October 2008 *Gourmet*, in which El Charro was named one of "America's 21 Most Influential Restaurants." The designation has as much to do with Flores as it does with Flin, who died in 1972.

In spite of the growth of El Charro, healthful additions to the menu and the national acclaim, Monica Flin's spirit can still be felt in the charming dining room on Court Street.

## Rincon Market (1926)

What started out as a tiny neighborhood market near the campus of the University of Arizona is now a large deli/restaurant/grocery store/meeting place/wine-beer bar.

Jack Uvodich ran the market with his wife. But in the late 1960s, the university closed off streets that allowed access to the store. Claims and counterclaims ensued, but the Uvodiches lost. Their son decided to move the entire business to the south-side campus on Sixth Street in a building designed by Merritt H. Starkweather, a prominent Tucson architect.

Paul Cisek bought the market in 1975 and began changing the whole concept. In addition to the market, he added a fishmonger, butcher, deli, grill, food specialty area and tables and chairs so people could eat on-site. In 2007, Cisek sold Rincon Market to Ron and Kelly Abbott, who continue to grow the business. Customers often include UA coaches and their recruits. Sandwiches are named after many members of the coaching staff. Live music is a part of the scene. Writing groups and other gatherings meet there on a weekly basis. Rincon Market is truly a neighborhood hot spot.

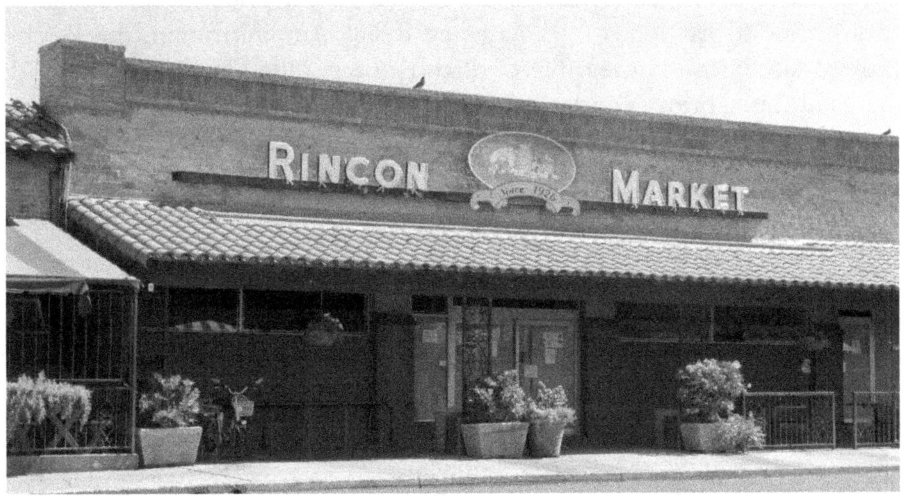


Rincon Market opened as a little neighborhood market in the 1930s. *Creative Commons, Max Pixel.*

# 1930s

## *Population: Tucson, 32,506; Pima County, 55,676*

As with most things, the Great Depression took a little longer to reach Tucson.

The tourist industry was still busy. In a speech to the American Automobile Association, the *Arizona Daily Star*'s editor reported that an average of 3.2 visitors arrived every day, spending a whopping five dollars each.

*Tucson: Official City & County Magazine* painted a rosy picture of the city in the early 1930s. Construction was still strong, with homes, schools and hospital additions going up at a rapid pace. The Fox Theatre, a federal building, the Montgomery Ward Store and numerous churches all became a part of the Tucson cityscape. Before the crash, bonds had passed for improving streets, parks and other public areas. Later in the decade, though, articles in this monthly magazine published by the Tucson Chamber of Commerce centered more on tourist attractions in order to entice visitors. Nonetheless, Tucsonans were affected in numerous ways once the national banks closed and people began migrating west looking for work.

Civic groups and concerned citizens stepped up to the plate. Employment services, job development, financial assistance and help with health and housing were established by ordinary citizens and various local social service organizations. All of that helped, as did a variety of federal projects. One was the building of Sabino Canyon, which today is a popular tourist attraction. The focus was to secure more water for the city. While that aspect never really came to fruition, the Emergency Relief Administration, the Works Project Administration and the Civilian Conservation Corps (CCC) paved the road, built bridges and created campgrounds to make the area more accessible. The CCC also helped build the Mount Lemmon Highway.

The movie industry discovered Tucson and built Old Tucson Studios. The city began an ambitious parks program, and tourists found their way to Tucson.

The options for dining out were limited. Minority ownership wasn't uncommon, and cafés and diners acted as community centers for new immigrants. Mexican restaurants were plentiful, but Italian food began to appear. One place, the Original Mexican and Italian Restaurant, proudly boasted serving both. Downtown was the epicenter of good eats that appealed to both merchants and shoppers.

Things started looking up by the middle to late 1930s, and Tucson was on the road to recovery.

## Arizona Inn (1931)

The Arizona Inn was opened by Isabella Greenway, a most remarkable woman. She was Arizona's first woman in the U.S. Congress and a bridesmaid at Franklin and Eleanor Roosevelt's wedding. She had managed a 130,000-acre ranch, was widowed twice, raised a family and, in 1927, established a workshop where injured World War I veterans were trained to make furniture.

The inn is the real story, but many people in Tucson have fond memories of the dining room, with its posh ambiance and impeccable service. When the Arizona Inn opened, there were twenty-seven employees in the kitchen alone. Items on early menus included fruit cups, baby lobster in cream, roast tom turkey and assorted vegetables. Desserts ran the gamut from peach melba to prune whip. It drew high praise from as far away as the *Chicago Tribune*. Dining at the Arizona Inn is still a special occasion.

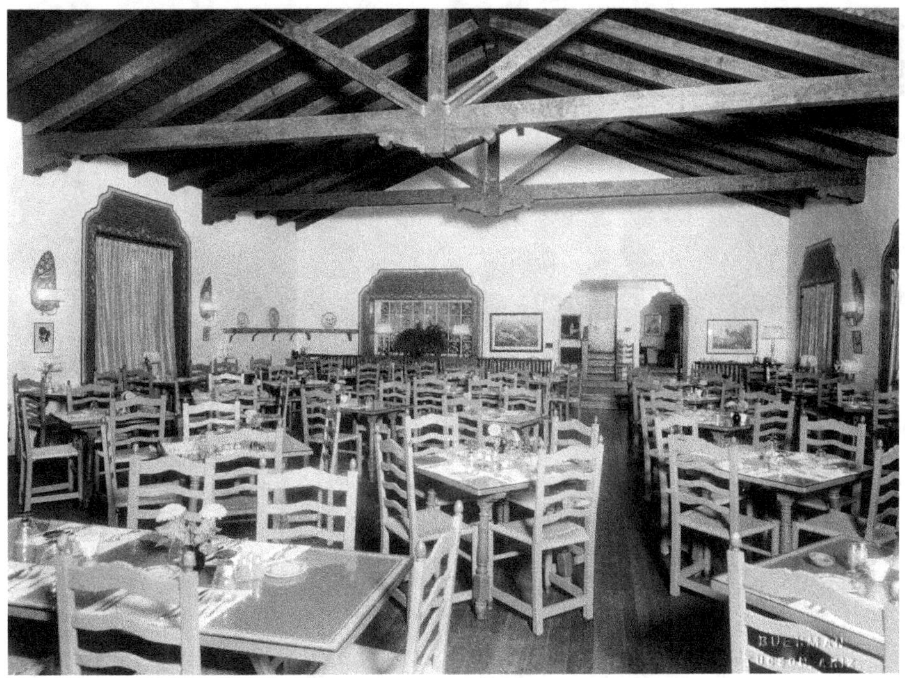

The Arizona Inn dining room. *Courtesy Arizona Inn.*

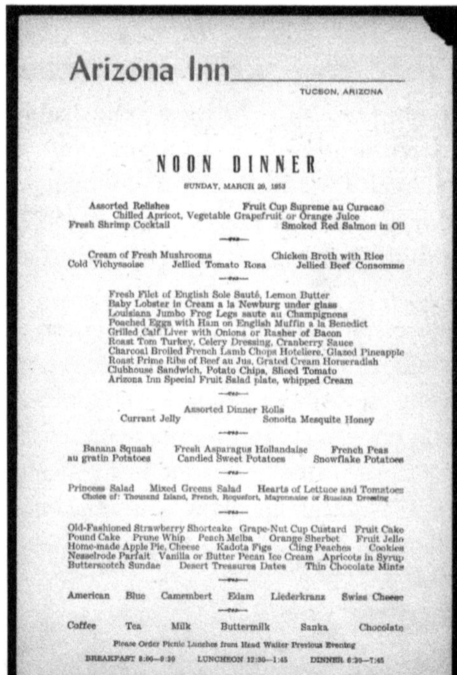

Arizona Inn

TUCSON, ARIZONA

NOON DINNER

SUNDAY, MARCH 29, 1953

Assorted Relishes — Fruit Cup Supreme au Curacao
Chilled Apricot, Vegetable Grapefruit or Orange Juice
Fresh Shrimp Cocktail — Smoked Red Salmon in Oil

Cream of Fresh Mushrooms — Chicken Broth with Rice
Cold Vichyssoise — Jellied Tomato Rosa — Jellied Beef Consomme

Fresh Filet of English Sole Sauté, Lemon Butter
Baby Lobster in Cream a la Newburg under glass
Louisiana Jumbo Frog Legs saute au Champignons
Poached Eggs with Ham on English Muffin a la Benedict
Grilled Calf Liver with Onions or Rasher of Bacon
Roast Tom Turkey, Celery Dressing, Cranberry Sauce
Charcoal Broiled French Lamb Chops Hoteliere, Glazed Pineapple
Roast Prime Ribs of Beef au Jus, Grated Cream Horseradish
Clubhouse Sandwich, Potato Chips, Sliced Tomato
Arizona Inn Special Fruit Salad plate, whipped Cream

Assorted Dinner Rolls
Currant Jelly — Sonoita Mesquite Honey

Banana Squash — Fresh Asparagus Hollandaise — French Peas
au gratin Potatoes — Candied Sweet Potatoes — Snowflake Potatoes

Princess Salad — Mixed Greens Salad — Hearts of Lettuce and Tomatoes
Choice of: Thousand Island, French, Roquefort, Mayonnaise or Russian Dressing

Old-Fashioned Strawberry Shortcake — Grape-Nut Cup Custard — Fruit Cake
Pound Cake — Prune Whip — Peach Melba — Orange Sherbet — Fruit Jello
Home-made Apple Pie, Cheese — Kadota Figs — Cling Peaches — Cookies
Nesselrode Parfait — Vanilla or Butter Pecan Ice Cream — Apricots in Syrup
Butterscotch Sundae — Desert Treasures Dates — Thin Chocolate Mints

American — Blue — Camembert — Edam — Liederkranz — Swiss Cheese

Coffee — Tea — Milk — Buttermilk — Sanka — Chocolate

Please Order Picnic Lunches from Head Waiter Previous Evening

BREAKFAST 8:00—9:30 — LUNCHEON 12:30—1:45 — DINNER 6:30—7:45

*Left*: Arizona Inn lunch menu, circa 1950. *Courtesy Arizona Inn.*

*Below*: Prepping for service. *Courtesy Arizona Inn.*

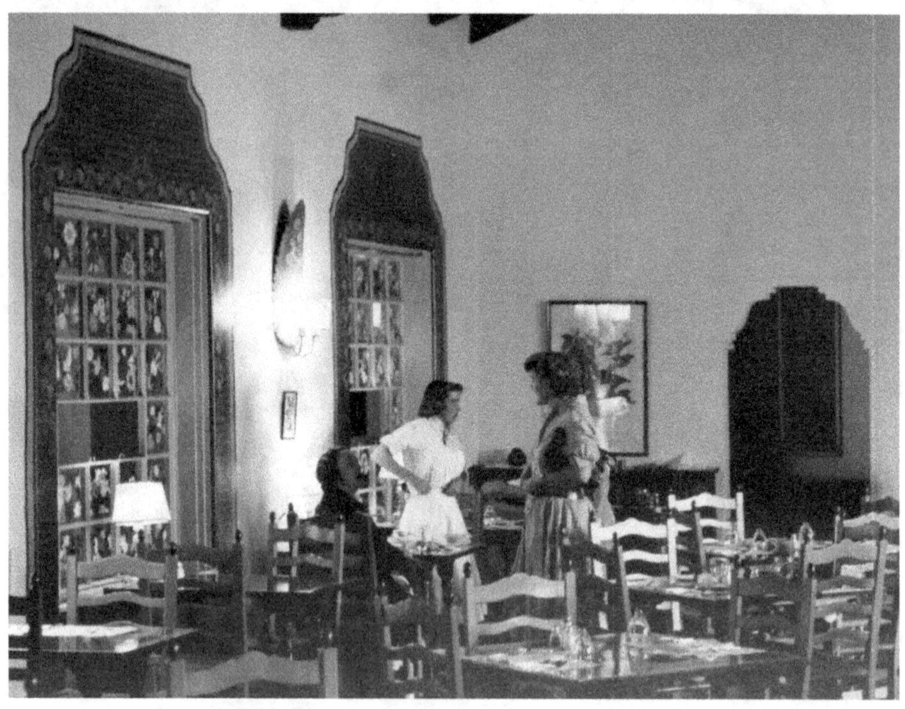

## El Minuto (1936)
## From an Interview with Teresa Shaar

The name *El Minuto* came about when original owner John "Juan" Shaar boasted that diners could get their burros in a minute. Of course, the menu was considerably smaller in 1937, when Shaar first opened the doors to his restaurant. Located on Congress Street west of downtown, El Minuto was relocated a mile or so away when I-10 was built. The family home was next door.

Originally from Lebanon, Shaar came to Tucson via El Paso, which is where his son George was born. He had a restaurant there, and he loved Mexican food, so it was only logical that when he moved to the Old Pueblo he would open a Mexican restaurant.

George Sr. met his wife, Rosalva Lopez, in Nogales, Sonora. Since El Minuto was a family restaurant, the young couple worked together there from the early days of their marriage. Juan's granddaughter Teresa Shaar said the menu had only a limited menu: menudo, tacos, burros, beans and maybe a few other items. Rosalva added her own recipes to the mix.

In 1944, the business was forced to move when I-10 was built. It relocated about a mile or two east, next to the family home in Barrio Viejo. In the early 1970s, their home had to be torn down when the Tucson Convention Center (TCC) was built. Oddly, the restaurant, located right next door, was saved, as were all the houses across the street.

The TCC became both a blessing and a curse for business. During its construction, people had a difficult time finding El Minuto, and when Main Street was rerouted to make way for the TCC, people thought the restaurant had closed. Business became so bad that George Sr. took a second job to support the growing family and keep the restaurant open. The family persisted because, Teresa said, her father was a good businessman and "We love the restaurant business." On the positive side of having a neighbor like the TCC, both the audiences and acts dine at the restaurant after concerts. Everyone from ZZ Top to Liberace to Oscar de La Hoya stopped by. Teresa remembers Liberace as a really nice guy.

The Shaars also operated a restaurant in Green Valley, a small town between Tucson and Nogales, Arizona. They called it Los Amigos and used the same recipes and food from El Minuto. George Sr. and his wife ran the Green Valley site with a partner while George Jr. and Teresa manned El Minuto. George Sr. was driving back from Green Valley when he was killed in a car accident.

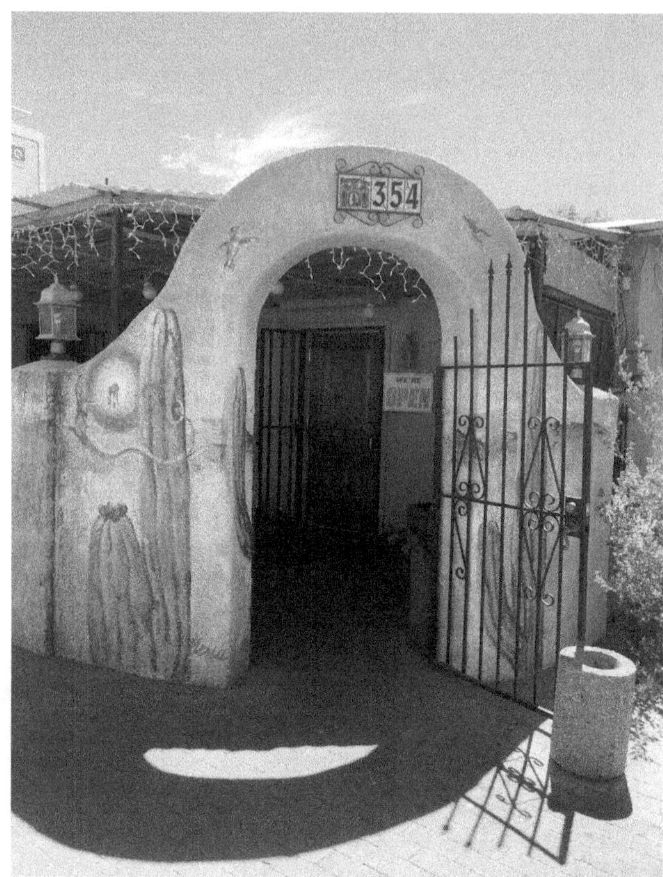


*Left*: The outside walls of El Minuto greet you with color. *Author photo*.

*Below*: The Wishing Shrine. Light a candle, make a wish. If your candle lasts the night, your wish will come true. *Wikicommons*.

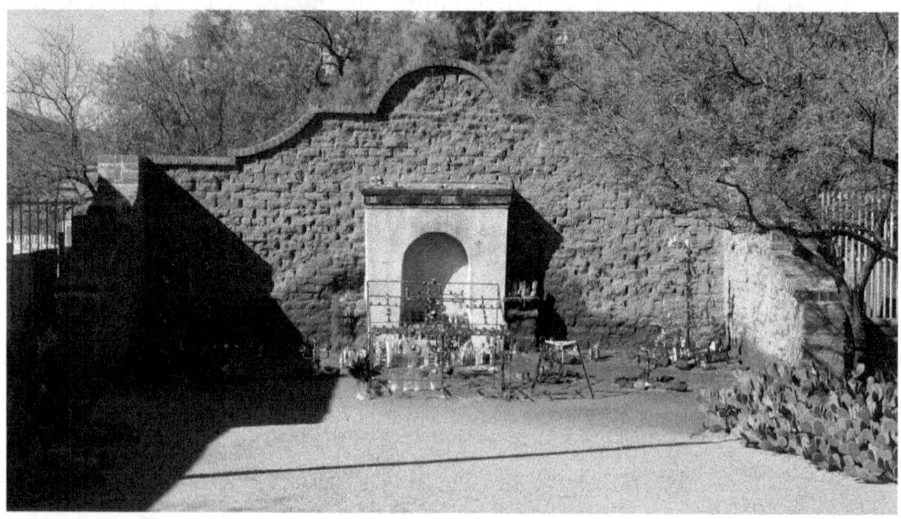

Rosalva was bought out by the partners and concentrated her efforts on the Tucson restaurant. Until her retirement in April 2017, she could be found there, usually behind the cash register.

Teresa had her own branch of El Minuto in midtown from 1996 through 2006, but competition from chains and the economy forced her to close. She returned to El Minuto, for which Tucsonans are most grateful.

Another neighbor that brings in travelers is El Tiradito Wishing Shrine. The space is small and can be easily missed, but because it is in the National Register of Historic Places, tourists stop by daily. The story of El Tiradito is of a tragic love triangle involving the murder of Juan Oliveras. The legend says his body could not be buried in a Catholic cemetery due to his part of the triangle, so his lover buried him on her property and built a shrine. No matter that the shrine has been moved several times; if a visitor lights a candle, makes a wish and the candle is still burning in the morning, the wish will come true.

The family added a dining room where the house once stood and decorated the whole space with desert colors, bright Mexican trinkets and artwork. The shaded patio accommodated more tables.

George Jr. died in 2016, and Rosalva retired. Teresa, her brother Michael and her daughter Zulema Salinas now manage all aspects of the restaurant. So, a fourth generation continues the family Sonoran-style recipes.

"It's simple, but it tastes good," said Teresa. "And we're still pretty fast, don't you think?"

## CROSSROADS (1936)
### FROM AN INTERVIEW WITH ARACELY GONZALEZ

Not much information is available about the early days of Crossroads Drive-In. Opened in 1936, the tiny drive-in was one of the earliest restaurants on what is now South Tucson's Restaurant Row. But newspapers didn't cover restaurants like they do today.

The first news was in an article in the *Arizona Daily Star* in 1977 featuring Mexican restaurant options. The article was short, noting that the owners, Dick and Alyce Fultz, had owned Crossroads for fourteen years. The cook commented that chimis are the big seller because "they go well with beer." It also stated that the Fultzes added Mexican food to the menu and that a good day could bring in four hundred customers. The house specialty, the Gizmo, a Crossroads invention (a large tortilla

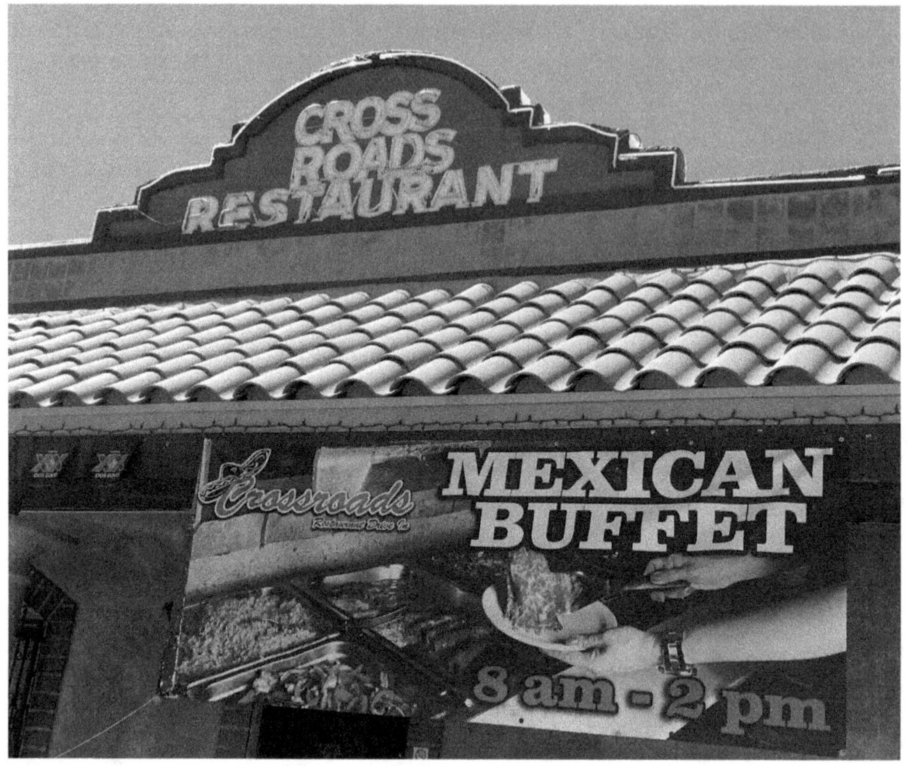


Crossroads Drive-in is one of the oldest restaurants in South Tucson. *Author photo.*

filled with cheese, folded and grilled) was mentioned. And that was all the article included.

While the Gizmo is still on the menu, as well as burgers and fried chicken, Crossroads has undergone many changes. My earliest memories include going to the drive-in for a burro and a pitcher of beer. That may sound pretty ordinary, but what made it stand out was that the pitcher of beer was brought to the car just like root beer at A&W. I'm not sure if that was before or after the Gonzalez brothers, Roberto Sr. and Antonio, purchased Crossroads, but I do remember being delighted at the whole idea.

Nights were big at Crossroads. Located just across the street from the now-defunct Greyhound racetrack, the restaurant attracted the winners and losers from the track. Couples would come after a night of dancing at nearby ballrooms. Soccer and baseball fields were in the neighborhood, and families always found their way there. On Sundays, it was a go-to place after church.

Parents could hang out in the cars or at picnic tables on the patio. Kids could play freely. On certain nights, there was live music. Teens could hang out, perhaps meet their future spouses over a burro. Dining at Crossroads was a social event with something for everyone.

Roberto Sr. took over sole ownership in 1982. His brother went on to another restaurant in South Tucson. Roberto then sold the place to his nephew Roberto in 2001. Roberto, also called Bobby, has worked at the restaurant since he was five years old. Today, he and his wife, Aracely, own and operate the historic eatery.

The menu contains old family Sonoran dishes with some additions of Aracely's recipes. Choices include plenty of seafood and other traditional Sonoran fare. The salsa has won "Best Salsa" in numerous contests around town.

Bit by bit, the young Gonzalezes enclosed the patio and refigured the space, so now all dining is done inside bright, colorful rooms. People don't seem to mind.

As generations continue to dine at Crossroads, they tell their stories. One woman visited after her husband's funeral and told Aracely that she had met her husband there and that Crossroads was "their place." Others talk about eating at Crossroads with their parents while their grandchildren listen. On the seventy-fifth anniversary in 2011, Roberto and Aracely brought back the Crossroads of an earlier time with live music, dancing in the parking lot and plenty of food.

And while Aracely and Roberto's children are still too young to take over the business, they can often be found pitching in as they can and carrying on the family traditions.

## CARUSO'S (1938)
## FROM INTERVIEWS WITH SAL ZAGONA SR., SAL ZAGONA JR. AND ANDE MOTZKIN IN 2017

An old Sicilian adage claims that "good fortune in life is tied to rain."

In 1938, when Nicasio Zagona got off the bus in Tucson to stretch his legs and saw it was raining, he took it as a sign of good luck and decided to stay. Originally from Palermo, Zagona was on his way to San Diego. Suffering from respiratory issues, he had been advised to move from Brooklyn to a warmer, drier climate. With every intention of settling in Southern California, he heeded the rain and decided not to get back on the bus. The

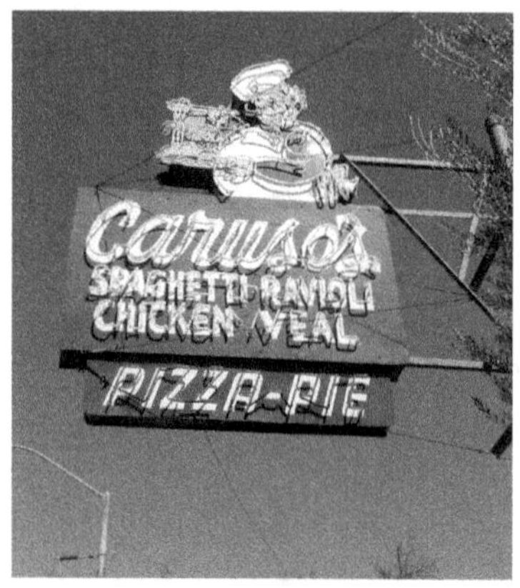


The famous Caruso's neon sign can be seen for blocks. *Author photo.*

decision brought good fortune to him and to Tucson.

The Depression was in full swing, and work was hard to find. Zagona hit upon the idea of selling food of his heritage. He persuaded a saloon owner to give him a small space in the bar where he would serve Italian dishes; both parties would make a little money. He met with quick success. He moved on to larger bars around town, and he soon had enough money to open his own place. He found a space on Fourth Avenue and named it after the famous Italian tenor Enrico Caruso.

Shortly after the move, rain changed his life again. During one of Tucson's famous August monsoon rains, Zagona was at the restaurant and headed outside to check for any damage the heavy rains had caused. As he stepped outside, the walls collapsed. He narrowly escaped serious injury.

He moved his restaurant to higher ground a block north but still on Fourth Avenue. It is where Caruso's still stands today as Fourth Avenue's longest-running restaurant. The new site, a duplex, had once been a Mexican restaurant (El Charro) and an electrician's shop. There was space for a tiny restaurant and decent living quarters.

Through the war years, the restaurant did well, but the postwar economy lagged, as did the business. In 1946, Zagona's son Salvatore, recently discharged from naval duty in the South Pacific, came for a visit. He was charmed by Tucson and thrilled to be enjoying the wonderful food prepared by his father. He decided to stay for a time.

Sal worked at the *Arizona Daily Star* as a proofreader and began attending the University of Arizona, where he would eventually earn a doctorate in psychology. He began working with his father at the restaurant. But business was bad, and Nicasio wanted to retire. In 1949, he decided to sell the restaurant. Hearing the news, Sal realized he had to do something, especially since the sale was happening at that very moment. That year, Sal also met and married his wife, Ingeborg Aas, also known as Teddy. The marriage lasted sixty-eight years and produced six children.

Sal leased the restaurant from his father in 1950 and, in 1952, bought it outright. In the early years of Sal's ownership, business was slow. But he

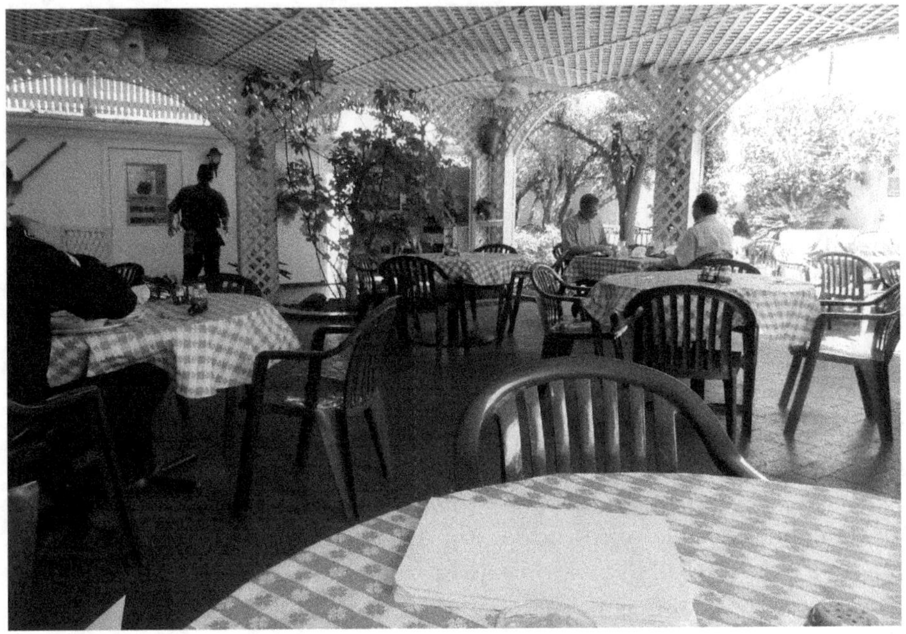

The patio at Caruso's is like a little bit of Italy. *Author photo.*

persevered, all the while teaching at the university, becoming a professor and raising six children. He credits the success to his wife, siblings, children and loyal employees. All of the family members worked at the restaurant over the years.

Sal converted the apartment side of the building into another dining room. The decor changed. Murals by Jose De La Flor graced the walls. Red checkered tablecloths covered the tables. The patio, which had a fountain, Italian Cypress trees and old-growth fruit trees, was expanded.

Lasagna, a dish not found anyplace else in Tucson, appeared on the menu. The fettuccine Alfredo, from a recipe of longtime hostess/cook Pat Hart, became a staple. Hart was also responsible for perfecting the house salad dressing and restaurant operations.

In the 1970s, Fourth Avenue was experiencing growing pains, but Caruso's held steady. Many of the old-time customers were now bringing their children to Caruso's, who then brought their children. The place was popular with the college crowd. Lee Marvin, who lived in Tucson, was a regular.

In recent years, Sal Sr. stepped back a bit, and a third generation of Zagonas, Sal Jr., became manager. Known as Whitey, he's done every job at the restaurant. He added his own touches. And today, there is a fourth generation—Andrea, Ande Motzkin. Ande's father was Sal Sr.'s brother, who owned the longtime restaurant Vince's in midtown. These days, Sal Sr. is still president of the company and plays an active role.

Whitey and Ande are vital to the success of Caruso's, but they both look to the past for their inspiration. Whitey attributes Caruso's continuing appeal to his dad. "He is most here in the atmosphere, particularly the patio. My father established the decor, the appearance, the feel of the place inside."

Motzkin adds: "For me the legacy is the thrill. Caruso's has so much soul. I love hearing the stories people tell me. 'We had our first date here.' 'My wife first told me she was pregnant while we were eating here.' 'My father loved this place, so we're having his funeral here.' It goes on and on." That sentiment is also true of the way Caruso's still operates. Many of the pastas are homemade. The sauce recipes are the same Nicasio created. Some of the staff have worked there for decades.

Monsoon season occurs every summer, still bringing good luck to the Zagona family and all generations of Tucsonans who dine at Caruso's.

## El Corral (1939)
### From an Interview with Dan Bates and Casey Wills

There's nothing really fancy about El Corral, and that's the charm. Known these days for prime rib and cowboy fixings, this restaurant dates back to a time when traveling by horseback was not uncommon and the idea of living so far away from town was considered foolish. Developer John Murphey thought differently. His purchase of eight thousand acres in the foothills created plenty of noise from the local press.

The *Tucson Citizen* mocked Murphey, noting that the land was practically useless and certainly not worth the fifteen dollars an acre he had paid. The year was 1915, and Murphey had plans to attract a certain group of people back east. He and Josias Joesler, who would soon become Tucson's premier architect, went on to prove his detractors wrong. Within ten years, the area was booming with new homes and new people.

Their partnership lasted for decades as Murphey built numerous structures throughout Tucson and Joesler became known for his Spanish Colonial Revival style. Although he designed numerous business structures, today, the homes Joesler created are sought after and demand a pretty price.

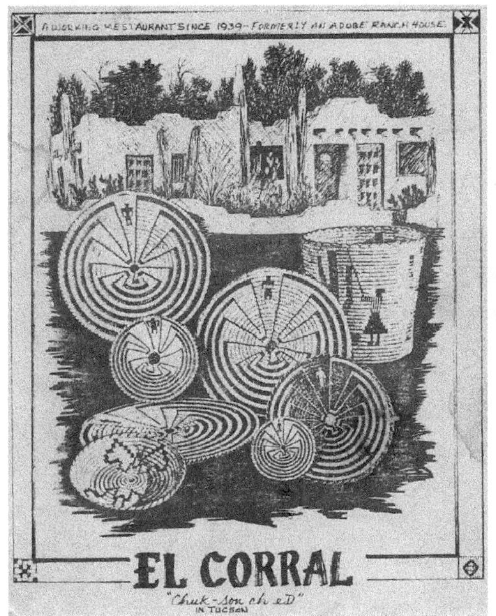


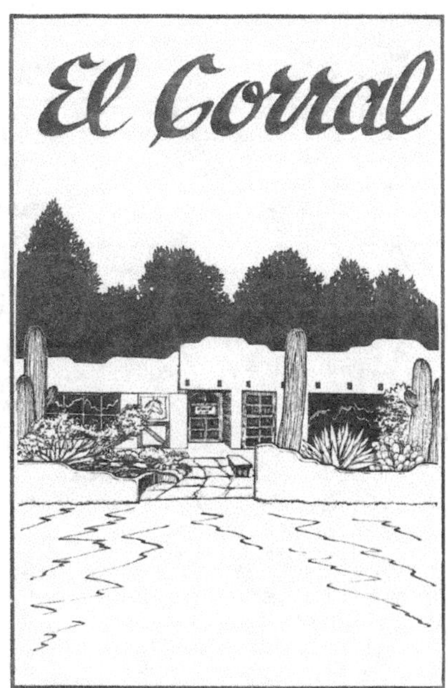


*Left*: The cover of a 1975 El Corral menu. *Courtesy Agro Land & Cattle Company.*

*Right*: Menu from El Corral, circa 1985. *Courtesy Agro Land & Cattle Company.*

As more homes were being built, the area needed businesses, so a restaurant was built along River Road. Called the El Corral Café, people say it was the first restaurant east of Oracle Road. By 1939, the café's owner, Leroy C. Perkins, subdivided the property and built small guest cottages for a guest ranch. With the catchy name Los Ranchos Perkins, the dude ranch attracted guests from all over the country.

A second owner, E.H. Bruening, changed the style and the name of the restaurant in 1946. The café was now El Corral Nightclub. Little is known about the nightclub, but sometime in the 1960s, the restaurant was sold to Dean Short, who owned some of Tucson's finest restaurants. Under his ownership, the restaurant thrived. The popular dishes of the decade were served: steaks, lobster and shrimp.

There is no record as to when Short sold the place to a Thomas Chandler. Chandler sold El Corral to Agro Land & Cattle Company in 1975. With the change in ownership came the change that would make El Corral famous. "We created the first prime rib house in Tucson," said Dan Bates, CEO of Agro Land & Cattle Company. "It took off like gangbusters."

El Corral Entrees

ROAST PRIME RIB OF BEEF AU JUS
SPECIALTY OF THE HOUSE

GENEROUS CUT . . . . . . . . . . . . . . 7.95
LARGE CUT . . . . . . . . . . . . . . . . 8.95
GRILLED CUT . . . . . . . . . . . . . . . 8.95
ENGLISH CUT . . . . . . . . . . . . . . . 8.95
PETITE CUT . . . . . . . . . . . . . . . 6.95
NOTE—PLEASE DISCUSS COOKING PREFERENCES WITH YOUR SERVER.

ADDITIONAL BEEF ENTREES

SOUTHWESTERN PEPPERCORN STEAK 7.95
T-BONE STEAK . . . . . . . . . . 7.95
N.Y. STEAK SANDWICH . . . . . . . . 4.95
STEAK PIE* . . . . . . . . . . . . 3.95
GROUND SIRLOIN SANDWICH* . . . . . 2.95

OTHER SELECTED OFFERINGS

BBQ PORK RIB COMBINATION 1/2 RACK WITH NEW YORK PETITE STEAK or PRIME RIB. 9.95
BBQ PORK RIBS..FULL RACK . . . . . . . . . 9.95
BBQ PORK RIBS..HALF RACK . . . . . . . . . 6.95
SALMON FILLET* . . . . . . . . . . . . . . 6.95
GRILLED HALIBUT . . . . . . . . . . . . . 6.95
TODAY'S CHICKEN* . . . . . . . . . . . . 6.95

* SIDE DISHES ON THESE ENTREES WILL VARY. PLEASE ASK YOUR SERVER. THANK YOU.

ENTREES INCLUDE CHOICE OF TAMALE PIE, MASHED POTATOES AND GRAVY, OR BAKED POTATOE WITH BUTTER OR SOUR CREAM. IN ADDITION, YOU MAY CHOOSE OUR SOUP OF THE DAY OR FRESH GARDEN SALAD. IF ALL MEMBERS OF THE TABLE AGREE...THIS DELICIOUS SALAD COMES "TOSSED TABLESIDE" WITH EL CORRAL'S OWN HONEY ITALIAN DRESSING...PLUS BREAD AND BUTTER.

NOTE: BEEF COOKED "WELL" DOES TEND TO LOSE SOME OF ITS NATURAL JUICES AND TENDERNESS. WE RECOMMEND CAUTION WHEN ORDERING.

*Left*: A menu from El Corral, 1975. *Courtesy Agro Land & Cattle Company*.

*Below*: The neon cowboy signals that you've arrived at El Corral. *Author photo*.

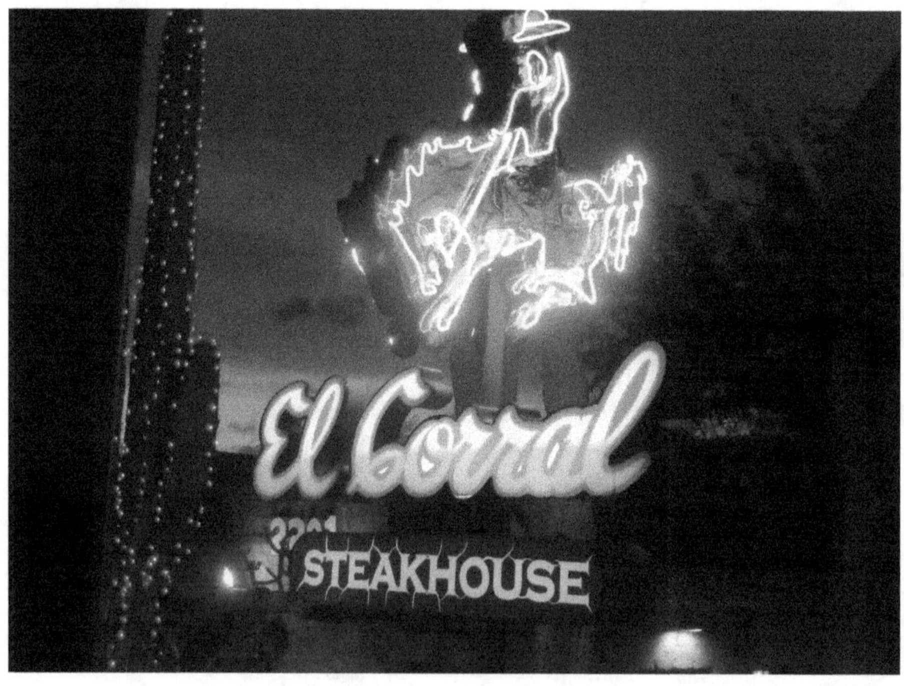

The original restaurant was in pretty good shape, so Agro kept it as the main dining room. Although it wasn't designed by Joesler, the room reflected his style, with large beamed ceilings, flagstone floors, thick adobe walls and heavy ornate doors. Large windows allowed for up-close views of the surrounding desert.

Only two cuts of prime rib were on the menu, a large and a small. The most popular side dish, the tamale pie, was also added to the menu. The pie has the consistency of a moist cornbread and is studded with corn, chiles and cheese. It was—and still is—the perfect complement to juicy prime rib. Other entrees, starters and sides were introduced as people's tastes changed. El Corral remains one of a few places in Tucson that serve Rocky Mountain oysters (aka fried bulls' testicles). Lest that be a deterrent, you can always finish the meal with the famous adobe mud pie.

Because a wait could be an hour or more, rooms were added. The additions are so well done that diners can't notice a difference. The decor screams Western history. You'll see a head-to-toe outfit once worn by Tom Mix, the "King of Cowboys." Cowboy art hangs next to old Western movie posters. Roy Rogers's boots are displayed. A photo of John Wayne is there, too. Saddles, spurs, cow horns, lanterns, big leather upholstered chairs, wooden tables and a flagstone fireplace add to the aura of an old, well-maintained ranch house.

Service is cowboy casual; there are no white linen tablecloths here. The bar is a holdover from a time when cocktails were cocktails. Everyone from families to people on a romantic date will feel comfortable here. It's a place that locals can take visitors to, and the visitors will return. Despite the fact that the dirt road out front is now a busy thoroughfare, the aura of the Golden West still lingers at El Corral.

# 3

# Bigger Bites

## 1940s–1950s

## 1940s

*Population: Tucson, 36,752; Pima County, 72,838*

As in most American cities, the war-at-home in Tucson was a busy time. The USS *Arizona* had been sunk in the attack on Pearl Harbor, and the connection to the battleship affected Arizonans deeply. Citizens did whatever they could to help the war effort. But bigger things were happening in Tucson to help America win the war.

In 1941, prior to America's entry into the war, Tucson's municipal airport became an army air base. Keeping the title Davis-Monthan, the base would serve as a training site for several bombardment groups. Civilians also worked on the base, assembling planes and parts. Rosie the Riveter was alive and well in Tucson. Ryan Field and a field in Marana were also training sites. At the municipal airport, Consolidated Vultie designed and built plane parts in its large wooden hangars. At the University of Arizona, more than eleven thousand men were trained; ten thousand of them were navy recruits. They slept on cots in Bear Down Gym. The navy, in 1942, won a contract to restore Old Main so that it could be used as a Naval Indoctrination School. Old Main, the first building on campus, had fallen into disrepair, rendering it unsafe.

After the war, returning servicemen and their families settled in Tucson by the thousands. Homes were needed, and construction increased. In 1948, Del Webb planned a development on what was then the edge of town. The goal was huge: 3,000 homes, the largest development between Los Angeles and Dallas. In the end, only 750 homes were built.

Tourism picked up. More people had cars, so travel was easier. Of course, Tucson benefited greatly. In 1948, there were 121 motor courts in the city. A *Chicago Tribune* article praised the merits of Tucson's dude ranches. Hollywood brought a steady flow of stars and crews to the area.

At midcentury, things were looking up for Tucsonans old and new.

## Casa Molina (1947)

Deciding on the most appropriate decade to place the Molina family restaurants is a bit tricky. While the original Casa Molina opened in 1947, it seemed that, in each succeeding decade, a Molina restaurant opened somewhere in Tucson and beyond. But let's start at the beginning.

In 1909, Francisco and Josefa moved to Tucson from Huepac, Sonora, Mexico, with their oldest children. They worked hard and eventually bought a ranch near Sabino Canyon, which at the time was far from the city proper. Their son Gilberto Molina, who was born in Tucson, worked for his dad but, as an adult, owned a construction company. When his sister Maria got divorced, he wanted to help, and he knew how he was going to do it. Because he loved his sister's food, he built Maria a restaurant. He did so literally, from the bottom up, including making all the adobe bricks himself. He called it Casa Molina. It had just sixteen seats. Gilbert even made those chairs and tables. These days, the restaurant sits on a very busy Speedway Boulevard and seats well over three hundred. Gilberto is also known for creating a taco maker, which accelerated the process of turning soft tacos crispy.

Because it was really the only Mexican restaurant on what was then the far east side, people flocked to the tiny spot, especially all the dudes at the nearby dude ranches. Some food, namely chiles, were grown on the family farm. Tortillas were made fresh every morning.

His brother Elias and Elias's wife, Louisa, helped out. In 1953, they opened their own place, calling it Molina's Midway, located, as the name implies, in midtown Tucson.

Eventually, Maria returned to Mexico; Gilbert and his family took over operations with his wife, Concepcion, doing the cooking.

Other restaurants followed. In 1965, a place was opened on Broadway (it was eventually sold to a corporation). Casa Molina del Norte (1966), which these days is located more midtown, is run by Gilberto Jr., who also oversees the Casa Molina on Grant Road. A branch in Nogales, Arizona, opened in 1967, run by Gilberto Sr.'s nephew Henry. There was a short-lived

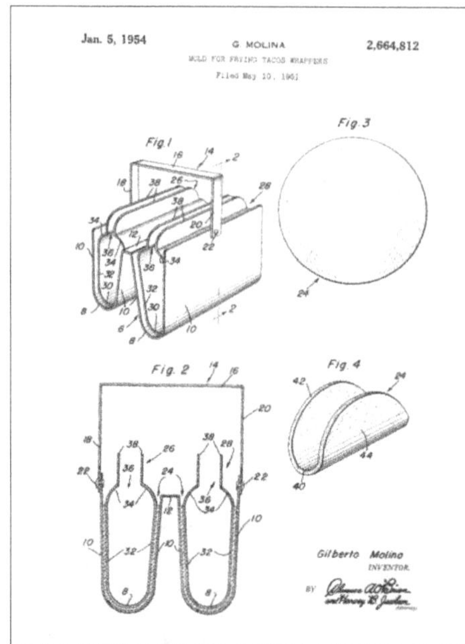


*Left*: Molina's patent for a better taco maker. *U.S. Patent Office.*

*Below*: Casa Molina del Norte is only one of many Molina family restaurants. *Author photo.*

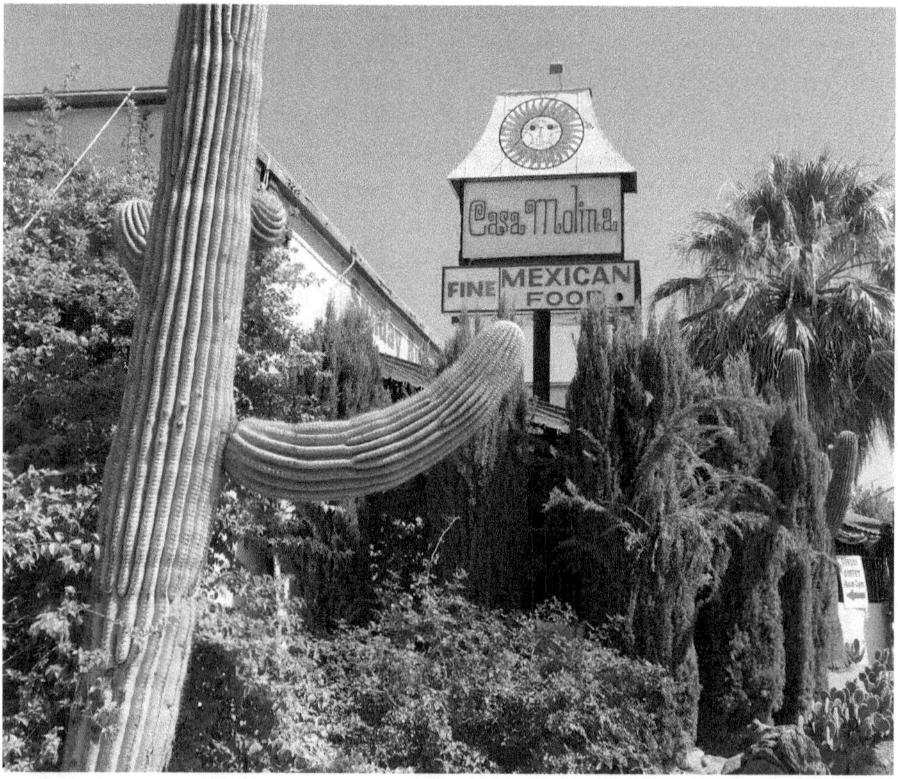

restaurant in Nogales, Sonora, Mexico. These were followed by El Molinito on the east side in 1978 and La Casita de Molina (1979) on the southwest side. An El Molinito on the far northwest side and another on the far east side are also part of the picture. Tillie, Elias and Louisa's daughter, owns two Las Margaritas restaurants, as well.

All the restaurants are operated by a cousin, a niece, a nephew or an in-law.

Many famous people ate at the Molina restaurants; Elizabeth Taylor, John Wayne and Charles Lindbergh were known to have dined at the original. Midway was a favorite of Paul and Linda McCartney when they lived in Tucson.

Sadly, as this book was being written, one of the oldest Molina restaurants, Midway Molina, closed. The kids of Elias and Louisa are all in their eighties and nineties, and the grandchildren felt it was time to move on.

Elias Sr. died in 1988. Louisa died in 1994. Gilberto Sr. died in 2003. The Molina family carries on the traditions begun sixty years ago in a tiny corner in the middle of nowhere.

## LI'L ABNER'S (1947)
### FROM INTERVIEWS WITH DAVE HOFFMAN AND CONNIE GILBERT

Say "Li'l Abner's" to longtime Tucsonans, and they'll speak of a time when driving there meant taking a long, dark, winding trip on a dirt road; of how the aroma of mesquite smoke signaled that you were approaching the restaurant; of where dining on a patio under the desert stars seemed like a trip back to the Golden West; and why, for some unknown reason, the steaks seemed bigger and juicier than all those places back in town.

The justification for the last claim is probably because they were. For decades, only two steaks were served at Li'l Abner's: the Large (a two-pound T-bone) and the Small (a one-pound porterhouse). Until about a year ago, there were no paper menus. All steaks came with ranch beans, Abner's salsa and cowboy toast. Dave Hoffman, the current owner, added other cuts of steak, ribs, chicken, fish, baked potatoes and salads to the menu.

The restaurant opened in 1947 as a bar. But there's something about the location that has attracted a crowd for decades. Cowboys liked to come together there for a cold beer and a bit of fun in the 1920s. Prior to that, in the 1820s, it was the site of a Butterfield Stage stop.

Larry Lewis, a local optician, and his wife, Duchess, a retired dancer who had worked in Hollywood, were the owners in the 1940s. The property was large enough for Lewis's business and a small home for Larry, Duchess and their dog, Abner. People remember Duchess for her glamorous clothes and her over-the-top personality.

Some say the Lewises served food. Other sources claim that it was only after the Lewises sold the restaurant in 1958 that the new owner, Lambert Kautenburger, added steaks to the menu and the huge patio grill, where the steaks were cooked over mesquite wood.

Old Tucson was in its heyday. Located just minutes from the movie studio, Li'l Abner's became popular with everyone from "The Duke" (John Wayne) to Lee Marvin and Marlon Brando. In later years, other stars, like Kris Kristofferson and Willard Scott, would often dine there whenever they were in Tucson. "We treated them like everybody else," said Hoffman, who bought the place in 1981. "They were just another customer."

Thanks to the large piece of land that the restaurant sits on, Kautenburger was able to add live entertainment, which, in the beginning, was roping contests with real cowboys. He sold the restaurant to Don Norman in 1963.

As with the question of when Li'l Abner's went from bar to restaurant, there is controversy as to when the stage and live music were added. Some say it was under Kautenburger's tenure; others credit Norman. But Norman's family did add a bit of the "Old West" to the story. His sons were arrested for stashing drug money on the property (among other nefarious activities). Regardless, the restaurant remained a popular spot.

Inside, wooden tables and benches are surrounded by a full regalia of cowboy gear. On the patio, in spite of all the strip malls located on either side of the grounds, dinner remains rustic.

Another controversy regards the numerous ghosts that seem to hang around the restaurant. While Hoffman can't attest to their existence, others will swear to hearing a little girl crying, lights turning on and off without anyone being there, objects being mysteriously moved or the appearance of George, the former maintenance man, sitting at the bar drinking his usual: a glass of milk.

Connie Gilbert, the bookkeeper who, with a handful of other employees, has been at the restaurant almost longer than Hoffman, tells the story about a visit from a former outlaw. One night, a woman was sitting at a table under a picture of Jesse James when she started screaming, "Someone is grabbing me by my waist!" Of course, no one was there, except perhaps the outlaw's spirit.

Today, Li'l Abner's still attracts crowds. Locals bring visiting guests to give them an Old West experience. Tourists travel from around the world to have a real mesquite steak like the cowboys used to do.

"We don't try and impress people with anything but the food," said Hoffman. "We have great food at a reasonable price and in a pretty neat atmosphere."

## THOSE STEAK JOINTS

As with most Western towns, Tucson has a full assortment of steakhouses. In recent years, chains have popped up offering massive cuts of midwestern corn-fed beef. But Tucsonans know and love their western beef. The steaks may not be as meltingly tender as the corn-fed variety, but no matter. We love them.

Each restaurant has a special twist or two, but meat offerings are similar and side dishes seldom vary: cowboy beans, a baked potato and a salad of some kind.

### CODY'S BEEF N' BEANS (1988)

Cody's is known for good, solid food at reasonable prices, all served in a cowboy casual setting. Mike Ferran was a butcher, and when he and his wife, Sandy, moved to Tucson, he decided to open a restaurant utilizing his skills. This was long before it became trendy for restaurants to cut and age their own steaks. Things haven't changed much since Cody's opened, except now the next generation is wielding the knives.

### SILVER SADDLE (1984)

The smoky aroma from decades of grilled meat lingers in the air. The Alva family has owned this south-side favorite since the beginning. The grill, which is located within diners' view, was built specifically for the restaurant. To help ensure that the steaks are cooked perfectly, the grill is attached to an antique buggy wheel and can be pulled up or down as needed. Only local mesquite wood is used. Recent visitors include Adam Sandler and Ben Carson, which proves that, at the Silver Saddle, everyone will feel at home.

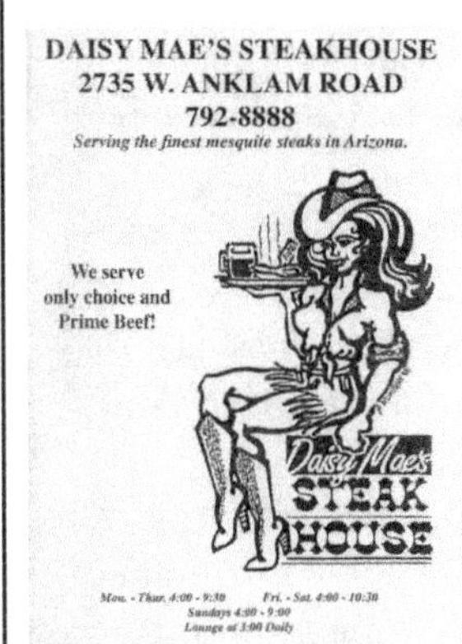


Daisy Mae's Steakhouse menu. *From the author's collection.*

### DAISY MAE'S (1990)

Back when Tucson was home to Major League Baseball spring training, Daisy Mae's was a favorite of many players. The UA basketball team has been known to dine there, too.

In the comics, Daisy Mae is Li'l Abner's true love. In Tucson, the two steakhouses are not related in any way.

The decor is created by customers, who write messages on dollar bills and then hang the money on the wall. Thousands of bills line the walls. They are taken down about every three or four years, and the money is donated to a local charity.

# 1950s

## *Population: Tucson, 45,454; Pima County, 141,206*

Midcentury Tucson was a busy place.

People, including former service members, were moving to the area in droves. They needed housing, jobs and entertainment. Construction employment boomed. Subdivisions sprang up outside the Tucson city limits. Lax building codes made it easier to meet demand.

The powers that be were a little slow in annexing additional land, but in 1953 alone there were ten separate annexations, and from 1952 to 1959, the city's area grew from 9.912 square miles to 48.856 square miles. The annexation continued throughout the 1960s and 1970s.

Certain groups of people objected. They didn't want Tucson to change or grow. But there was no stopping the juggernaut of people who wanted to live where it was warm, relatively inexpensive and naturally beautiful.

Construction of shopping centers was also part of the growth. People could now buy just about anything within blocks of their homes, regardless of what part of town they lived in.

Manufacturing jobs were plentiful. Consolidated Vultee, a major employer, moved out of town after the war, but others moved in. Most notably, Hughes Aircraft opened in 1951 and created thousands of high-paying jobs for decades. Other corporations relocated to Tucson, including Douglas Aircraft and Krieger Air Conditioning. The number of new companies increased 115 percent. Today, the Hughes campus is home to Raytheon Missile Systems and still employs hundreds of Tucsonans.

But it wasn't all big industry. Tucson, in keeping with an emphasis on tourism, was also home to ten clothing design businesses that created Western and resort wear, adding $8 million to the 1950 economy alone.

About those tourists—they just kept coming. Tourists visited the brand-new Arizona-Sonora Desert Museum, which opened on Labor Day weekend in 1952. They shopped at the new Levy's (1950) and Jacome's (1951) department stores downtown. They went to the rodeo and the movies. And, of course, they ate in restaurants.

But they weren't the only people spending money at local restaurants. With more leisure time and the advent of frozen and other convenience foods, attitudes about eating were changing. Families could dine in their cars at one of the many new drive-ins. Going out to dinner and dancing on a Friday evening was easier, thanks to bigger paychecks. Restaurants began advertising on that newfangled appliance, television.

These sociological changes were swift but would have long-lasting results.

## Mi Nidito (1952)
### From an Interview with Jimmy Lopez

Mi Nidito Mexican Restaurant almost wasn't. Back in the early 1950s, when Ernesto and Alicia Lopez arrived in Tucson from Sonora, Mexico, they knew they wanted to open their own food-related business. Ernesto wanted a tortilla factory; Alicia thought a restaurant would be a better idea.

The restaurant won out.

"It was the best choice, I think," said grandson Jimmy Lopez, who operates the restaurant now with his brother Ernesto Lopez III. Tucsonans agree, because a wait for a table on most nights can be more than an hour. Recently, Jimmy Lopez secured a license to serve liquor on the front patio, so the wait can be a bit more fun.

In 1952, when Mi Nidito opened, South Fourth Avenue was a dirt road, and there weren't nearly the number of Mexican restaurants lining the street. Mass-market advertising was almost nonexistent. In spite of a few rough early years, word of mouth made Mi Nidito a popular place. Alicia used her family recipes, which form the menu today.

Mi Nidito translates to "My Little Nest." With twelve seats, the place was indeed tiny. In 1959, fifty seats were added; in 1992, thirty-five more. Yet the restaurant still maintains a cozy feeling from those earlier times.

Mi Nidito is a perennial winner in local "best of" lists, winning in categories ranging from best tacos to best South Tucson restaurant. One

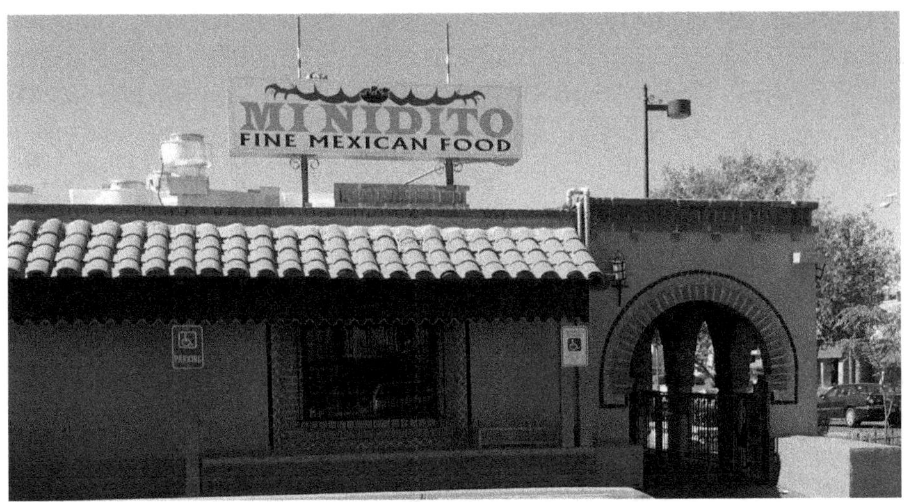


Celebrities seen at Mi Nidito include President Bill Clinton. *Author photo.*

year, it was named one of "America's Top 50 Mexican Restaurants" by *Hispanic* magazine.

Ernesto Jr. and his wife, Yolanda, who own Mi Nidito, retired recently. Jimmy credits his father, Ernesto Jr., who started working in the restaurant in the late 1950s, for growing the establishment. "My dad is the one who kept the place going," Lopez said. Ernesto retired after fifty-six years. He taught his sons the importance of hard work, honesty, respect and loyalty, especially when it comes to the restaurant.

Decor is a mix of "Aztec" drawings, beer signs, Christmas lights, silk flowers and knickknacks. The booths are wrapped in brightly striped serapes. Meals are delivered on carts. Photos of famous guests are also part of the decor: Willie Nelson, Julio Iglesias, ZZ Top, Jim Belushi, Graham Nash, David Crosby, Madeleine Albright and—oh, look, is that really Bill Clinton? It is indeed.

On February 25, 1999, while on a visit to Tucson, city officials brought President Clinton to Mi Nidito. "I never thought that would happen," joked Lopez. "When he sat down, he said, 'Put a big plate together for me because I'm really hungry.'" The plate consisted of a bean tostada, a chicken enchilada, a beef tamale, a chile relleno and one of the restaurant's signature birria tacos, in addition to beans, rice, guacamole, tortillas and a couple of slices of a cheese crisp.

Clinton made a point of greeting all of the customers in the restaurant. Lopez noted, though, that once the president sat down, no one else was allowed in. Even his grandmother, Alicia, the woman who had opened the restaurant, was made to wait on the front porch with all the other customers.

In the middle of the restaurant, there is the "President's Table." The five items Clinton ate are now a combo plate on the menu called, aptly enough, the "President's Plate." Adam Richman featured the dish on Food Network's *Man vs. Food* in 2009. Jane and Michael Stern, of *Roadfood*, called their meals at Mi Nidito "memorable," which is quite a compliment from people who eat for a living.

Jimmy joined the family business in 1971, and a good number of the staff who started with him are still around. The main chef, Maria, has been in the kitchen for forty-two years. A manager has been there for more than twenty years. Servers boast twenty and thirty years.

Customers have been coming here for decades, some as far back as when the bathrooms were outside. People who ate when Ernesto Sr. and Alicia were the only workers are now bringing their grandchildren.

Even though Mi Nidito is only open five days a week (Monday and Tuesday are used to catch up and power clean), it serves thousands of dishes every week. The kitchen makes 150 fresh-to-order chile rellenos a day. Anything with birria is a hot item. The chimichangas sell well, and the carne seca is a favorite.

Will the next generation continue the family business? Jimmy is doubtful, but he and Ernesto III will be involved as long as they can. They love their work and the restaurant. It's another lesson they learned from their father. "Take care of the restaurant, and it will take care of you."

If that's the case, Tucsonans will be enjoying Mi Nidito for years to come.

## LUCKY WISHBONE (1953)
### FROM INTERVIEWS WITH CLYDE BUZZARD AND MARK MORRIS

"It rained like you poured it out of a bucket," said Clyde Buzzard of Lucky Wishbone's opening night in July 1953. "We about drowned."

But the monsoon storm didn't deter hundreds of people as they stood in line to get a taste of the first "fast food" in Tucson. Offering a buy one, get one free, "Mom"-sized dinner might have helped draw the huge crowds. In the following weeks and months, lines out the door became a common sight.

When Derald Fulton opened Lucky Wishbone, no one had seen anything like it in Tucson. There were no tables, no servers and no tipping, People ordered at a counter and took their food home in a box or a bag. The menu was simple: fried chicken, fried shrimp and a couple of sandwiches. There were four sizes: Pop, Mom, Jr. and Family Feast. Tucsonans loved the food and the concept, and Lucky Wishbone was an immediate hit.

Fulton, a high school teacher and football coach in Illinois, moved to Phoenix in the 1940s. There, he opened the Polar Bar with a partner. When he moved to Tucson, he opened a Polar Bar there in 1948.

The Polar Bar was always busy but difficult to manage. Weekends found the parking lot full of rowdy teenagers, and there was both sit-down service and carhops.

"My uncle wanted something where people got food and left," said Fulton's great-nephew Mark Morris.

Fulton looked at what was happening in other parts of the country. Families were becoming more mobile. Drive-in theaters were popular. Home cooks were moving away from long, laborious meals as frozen foods and other time-saving methods became available. "He was a very smart man," said Morris. "He was on the cutting edge in the way that he thought."

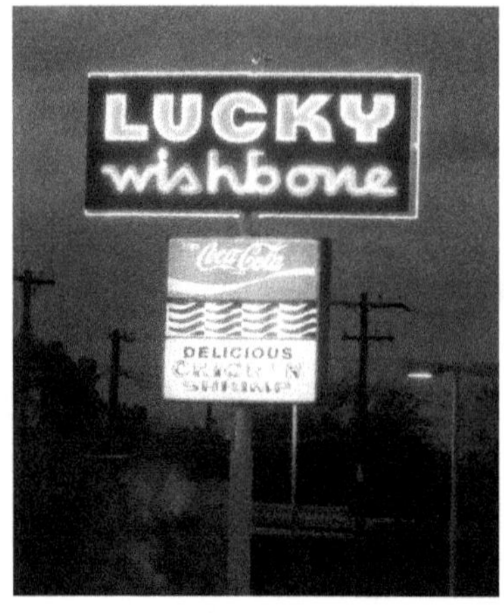


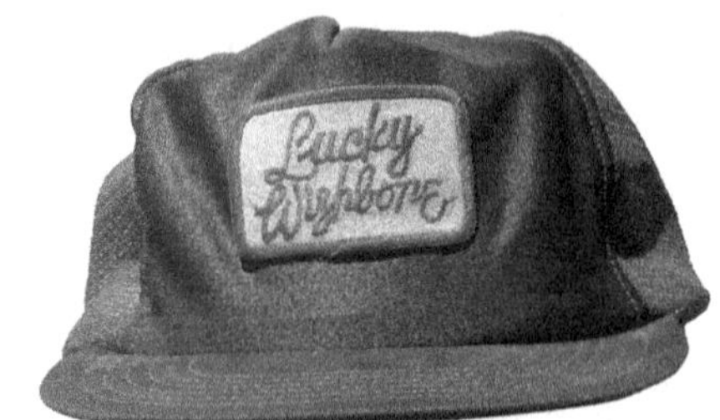


*Above*: Hat from Lucky Wishbone, circa 1978. *Courtesy Michael Suarez.*

*Left*: The sign from Lucky Wishbone lights up the desert sky. *Author photo.*

Buzzard, who worked at the Polar Bar as a dishwasher, recalled how, after work, Fulton and coworkers would share a few beers and talk about Fulton's idea for an easier way to serve good food.

Fulton offered Buzzard and another coworker, Donald Morris (Mark's father), the opportunity to partner with him on his new concept. The group decided to give it a go. Within months, the team—now joined by John Kinder—opened several more restaurants all over town. At the time, there was little, if any, competition. McDonald's wouldn't arrive in town for another eight years. The majority of restaurants only offered more formal sit-down service. The price point was unbeatable.

Lucky Wishbone became the place for families to go for a Sunday dinner or for the paper boy to stop on his way home from his route for a five-cent piece of Texas toast. "There was always a Lucky Wishbone nearby," said Buzzard.

Very little has changed at Lucky Wishbone. There are now steak fingers on the menu. "Nobody makes them like we do," says Morris.

Both Buzzard and Morris ascribe the longtime success to the quality of food and the loyalty of employees who worked for them for decades. "It's the quality" of the food, said Morris. "It starts out expensive for us." He also talks about employees. One helped open the store on Campbell Avenue in 1956 and worked there for fifty years. Buzzard hired women for their first jobs, and they stayed until retirement. "You're only as good as your employees," he said.

One of the most memorable symbols of Lucky Wishbone is the original neon sign that stands in front of the store on Swan Road. The giant blinking starburst can be seen for blocks. When Buzzard built a new store next door to replace the store built in 1954, he wanted to preserve the sign. Fortunately, about the same time, the Tucson Historic Preservation Foundation partnered with Pima Community College to preserve the neon signs that once were ubiquitous in Tucson. City codes limited how the sign could be preserved, but thankfully this symbol still glows in the night, welcoming one and all.

Kinder died in 1995, Donald Morris in 2008 and Fulton in 2011.

Now into its sixth decade, Lucky Wishbone has seven stores. Buzzard, the lone survivor at a spry eighty-six, runs two stores, as does Mark Morris. The other three are owned by the Jacobsen family, who bought into the company in 1995 after years of being a supplier with the company Arizona Sunland Foods.

In 1972, the local band Oracle (Fulton's son Gary was a member) recorded a jingle many people still associate with Lucky Wishbone. Written by Garry Rust, a local country singer, the song goes: "Looking for a place to remember. Just a place along the way…you'll find the Lucky Wishbone. You'll find the Lucky Wishbone." The song is no longer used, but somehow people still can find a Lucky Wishbone along the way.

## Pat's Drive In (1955)
### From an Interview with Gina Yturralde

Pat's Drive In has been called a city icon, a Tucson classic, a landmark eatery and humbly authentic. But when Henry "Pat" Patterson opened the first Pat's in 1955, those accolades certainly didn't even occur to him. Pat just wanted "to get people what they pay for." And he did just that.

Patterson came to Tucson much the same way many other people in this book did. He was basically passing through on an all-American road trip with his wife, Lynne. She was from England (although they met in Caracas, Venezuela, when Patterson was there working for Coca-Cola). They were on their way to the coast and had to stay in Tucson for a few weeks because Lynn needed to renew her visa. But then Tucson performed its magic, and the Pattersons decided to stay.

The first Pat's was located downtown on a plot of land Patterson purchased. In addition to the restaurant, the Pattersons owned two drinking establishments. The corner property he owned became a part of the great urban renewal project that changed the landscape of the downtown area. Unlike those who lost homes and businesses, Patterson profited from the sale and went on to open three other Pat's Drive Ins. Over the years, there was a

Pat's on East Speedway Boulevard, one on South Sixth Avenue and then one on North Grande Avenue, home to the current and only remaining Pat's. That site opened in 1961. The menu was small and simple: hamburgers and hot dogs, fried fish, chicken, shrimp, french fries and chili.

Pat's was the perfect place for the time. Teenagers had cars, and a drive-in that served inexpensive, greasy, delicious food was just what they wanted. Families, too, liked Pat's. Located in Barrio Hollywood, one of the many older neighborhoods in Tucson, Pat's also fit the needs of the working-class, mostly Mexican families who had lived there for generations. The family meal was perfect: seven dogs and fries for $1.30. By 1995, that same meal was still a deal at $5.95.

And while the hamburgers were popular, it was the chili dogs that made Pat's famous. Stories vary as to how Pat made his chili, but it didn't matter. You could order the chili hot or mild. A giant order of fries (which is still

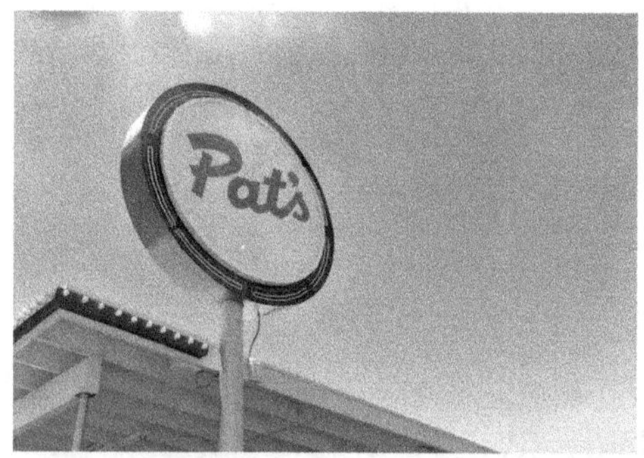


*Left*: Pat's sign is part of the Neon Pueblo Project created by the Tucson Historic Preservation Foundation. *Author photo.*

*Below*: Pat's is the place to go for chili dogs. *Author photo.*

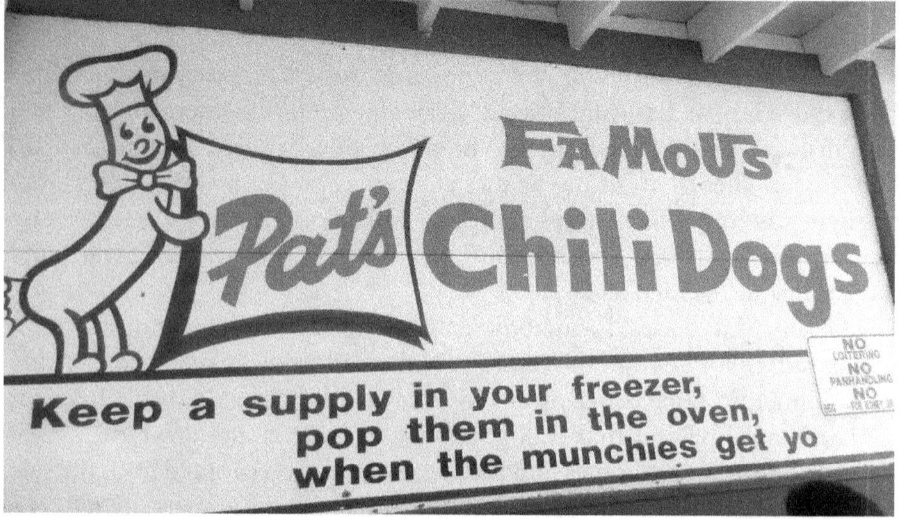

served in a brown paper bag that absorbs the wonderful greasiness Pat's is known for) was the perfect accompaniment.

Around 1963, Patterson hired a fifteen-year-old kid named Carlos "Charlie" Hernandez to help with cleaning up and other duties. He took Hernandez under his wing and became like a second father to him. Hernandez worked his way up the Pat's ladder.

In 1979, Patterson sold the place to Hernandez, because Pat's son Bruce had cancer. Pat wanted to spend time with his son. Sadly, Bruce died shortly after.

Hernandez's daughter Gina Yturralde remembers her entire family going to the Patterson home and watching home movies of the Pattersons' travels. She remembers Pat's handlebar moustache and his accent. "He told my dad, 'Maintain the business. Don't change anything and never go in with partners,'" Yturralde said.

Hernandez stuck with the advice, although for a while there were shakes on the menu. They were removed because "the employees were drinking up all the profits," said Yturralde. "They were that good." She also added that everything is the same as when Pat's first opened. "We just barely got new cash registers."

Patterson died in 1999 at the age of eighty-five.

People can still eat on one of the few picnic tables outside, indoors in a tiny dining room or in their car if they are lucky enough to get a parking spot in the small lot in front of the restaurant.

Pat's has been featured in *Maxim* magazine and is a space on the board game Tucson in a Box, a Monopoly-like game. Jane and Michael Stern wrote about the dogs and fries on their website, Roadfood.com.

Yturralde attributes Pat's continued success to the quality food, the quick service and the nostalgia. She said people have been coming to Pat's for decades and are now bringing their children and grandchildren. She added that some of the employees are the grandchildren of the original employees. "There's not any place like it in Tucson."

## Mama Louisa's (1956)

### From Interviews with Suzanne and Michael Elefante and Greg Casadei

While passing through Tucson on vacation from Detroit with her daughter, Mary Cicala, and family, Lugia "Louisa" Casadei fell in love with Tucson.

The warm sunny days and mountain views were reminiscent of her Italian hometown.

Bill, Mary's husband, was a carpenter. Work in Detroit was intermittent at best. Realizing Tucson's weather would make year-round work possible, he, Mary, Louisa and Ermino, her husband, moved to Tucson.

Louisa began working at an Italian restaurant, Pavone's. When Ida Pavone opened another restaurant, La Cocina, Louisa worked there. Louisa was making a pittance in spite of the fact that her recipes were what drew the crowds.

When her other son, Joe, visited, he wasn't happy seeing his mom's working conditions. He suggested she open her own place. Louisa wasn't sure at first, but within months, Joe and his family had moved to Tucson, and plans for her restaurant began. They bought property on the east side, at the time considered the boonies, but it was located at the main gate of Davis-Monthan Air Force Base, which would prove to be a huge customer base.

During construction, Bill's skills were invaluable. The whole family pitched in to build a tiny structure that would be called La Cantina. On February 29, 1956, the doors opened. Offering all those delicious dishes Louisa had made popular at La Cucina, the restaurant was a hit.

In 1957, the last of the Casadei family, Norino (Lottie), moved to Tucson. He and his family became part of the team. Now Louisa had everything she wanted. When customers asked if there really was a Mamma Louisa, Mamma would come out of the kitchen to charm the guests. "She was a big personality for a big woman," said her grandson Greg Casadei, "but in a kind way."

Over time, the name was changed to Mamma Louisa's Cantina. Murals by Basque artist Jose de la Flor graced the walls. A permanent bar replaced the tiny table in what had been the main dining room, called "La Padela." The name comes from all the frying pans serving as wall sconces. Photos of the sign out front and of menu covers show that La Cantina was renamed Mamma Louisa's Cantina, then Mamma Louisa's and eventually Mama Louisa's.

Dishes were added. Joe's Special began as a craving. Joe described what he wanted to eat: linguini, house red sauce, garlic butter, pepper flakes and melted cheese. The dish was so good that Mama added it to the menu. It remains a popular dish.

Mama Louisa's became a success. There was plenty of hard work to go around, but everyone, even all the kids no matter how old, did their share. The restaurant allowed them to bond in ways they couldn't have imagined.

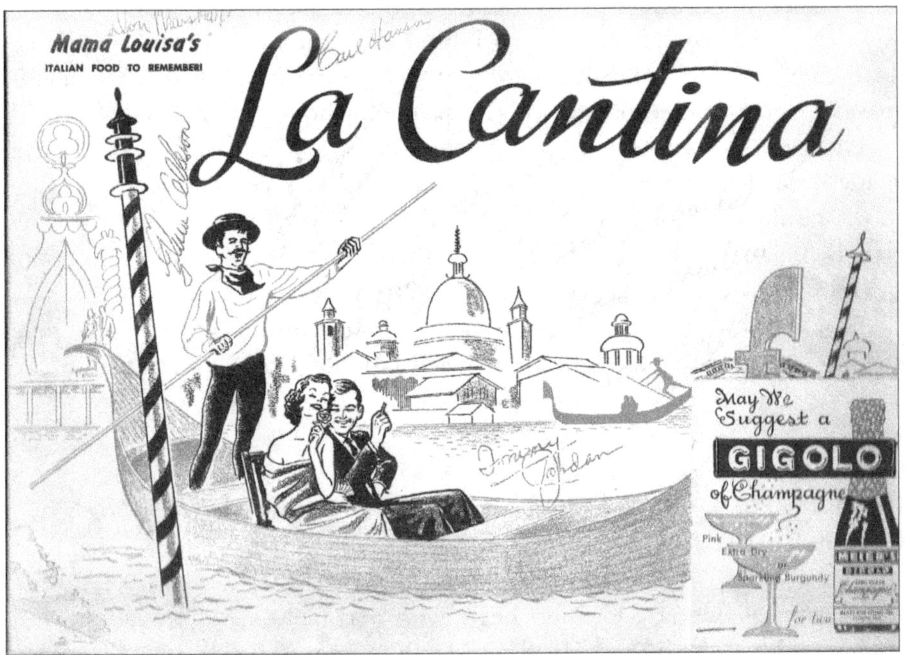


Mama Louisa's La Cantina menu. *Courtesy Michael Elefante.*

Around 1972, Bill was ready to retire. The family decided to sell. On a visit from Wantaugh, New York, Joe Elefante Sr. happened to have dinner at Mama Louisa's. When he found out the place was for sale, he bought it. His sister and brother-in-law, Louise and Sam Elman, were partners.

The Elefantes began to put their own mark on the restaurant. Jean, Joe's wife, cooked. While they maintained some of the original recipes (Joe's Special in particular), they also added family favorites, such as their Nonna's eggplant parmesan. As always, everything was made from scratch. They added tablecloths and moved walls and the hostess station. To-go orders were sent to the kitchen via a pneumatic tube. They kept the murals that had been so much a part of Mama Louisa's.

In 1974, son Joe Jr. and his wife, Suzanne, moved to Tucson from Miami, where Joe had been a graphic artist for the Miami Dolphins. Suzanne remembers her husband telling her he wanted to work with his dad. "My husband had a passion for cooking. He loved cooking," she said. Joe learned the recipes from his mom. Suzanne waited tables and acted as hostess. As kids (Joseph, Stacy and Michael) came along, they worked in various capacities. Aunts, uncles. cousins and friends were also a part of the mix.

In 1995, Joe Sr. retired and Joe Jr. and Suzanne became owners. Three years later, Joe Jr. died. Suzanne deftly took control. Today, son Michael is executive chef and co-owner with his brother, who lives in San Francisco.

The red sauce is made from scratch daily, and 120 pounds of pasta are made on a machine hooked up to a power drill. Michael takes great pride in the family tradition. He noted, "That's how I'm going to remember my dad, by being in the kitchen." He has added a "Third Generation Menu."

Guests, too, are third- and fourth-generation diners.

"The thing I like the most about being in a restaurant that has been here so long is that you see the guests and their families grow," said Suzanne.

## SAGUARO CORNERS (1956)

### FROM INTERVIEWS WITH FRANK CALVERT, SHERRY BARAN, JIM CAMPBELL, KADE MISLINSKI AND DAVE MUSSO

The stories of Saguaro Corners begin with Bert Calvert, who was sent west for his health at age fifteen. His sister Myrtle, whom he lived with, told him to "get a job." That order morphed into a life in heavy construction. He helped build dams, roads and trenches that made the Colorado River navigable in Yuma, Arizona. In Yuma, he became an integral part of the community, had a whirlwind marriage, divorced and obtained custody of his son Frank (an interesting story in and of itself).

In 1956, Bert came into a parcel of land on the edge of Saguaro National Park East, thanks to a partnership that never panned out. Using his knowledge and some clever ideas, he built a small enclave of buildings that consisted of a gas station, a small apartment and a burger stand. The restaurant had a counter and three or four tables. He called the stop Saguaro Corners.

Because work required travel, Bert leased the place to a variety of people and sent Frank to a military academy in California. Saguaro Corners was to be his retirement. When Frank was twelve, Bert decided it was time for his son to work in the family business and took him out of school. Over the years, Frank and Bert reconfigured and expanded the restaurant; built Rincon Ranch Estates, a small housing development in the area; and established a water company.

Frank married and moved to California. He and his wife, Florence, had three children, Dale, Bob and Sherry.

In 1963, on a trip to visit Frank, Bert wasn't feeling well and decided to fly home. He picked up his car at the Tucson airport, only to pull over a few minutes later and die of a heart attack. Frank and Florence left for Tucson immediately. When they arrived, they discovered that the people leasing the restaurant had left town in in the middle of the night, owing everybody money. Bert's death had been on the news; apparently, on hearing the news, they'd absconded. "Frank had to figure out what he was going to do with the place," said Dale. "It was either sell everything or take over the restaurant and run it." He decided on the latter.

Frank worked the kitchen, Florence worked the front of the house and the children worked where they were needed. Frank changed the dining area, moved the kitchen, added another dining room and developed a menu consisting of "food he liked to eat," said daughter Sherry Baran. Eventually, he also removed the gas pumps to avoid any contamination to the water table. Because he and Florence loved to sit and watch the abundant wildlife living in the area, he added huge picture windows. Diners could enjoy a live show featuring coyotes, raccoons, javelina pigs, birds, squirrels and more. The views became the restaurant's major attraction.

On Saturdays, there was prime rib; every other Sunday meant either roast leg of lamb with sour cream gravy or slow-cooked beef ribs. Steaks, lamb, spaghetti, Italian specialties, fried and broiled chicken, liver and onions and, on occasion, lobster were on the menu. Soups, salad dressings and sauces were made in-house. "Home cooked food with a gourmet touch" as the matchbooks proclaimed.

Frank was known for his gruff but loveable personality, his attention to detail, his incredible work ethic and his outstanding hospitality.

Dale became a CPA; Sherry worked at the university; Bob joined the air force; and Frank and Florence kept the restaurant going strong. Later, Sherry returned as the bookkeeper.

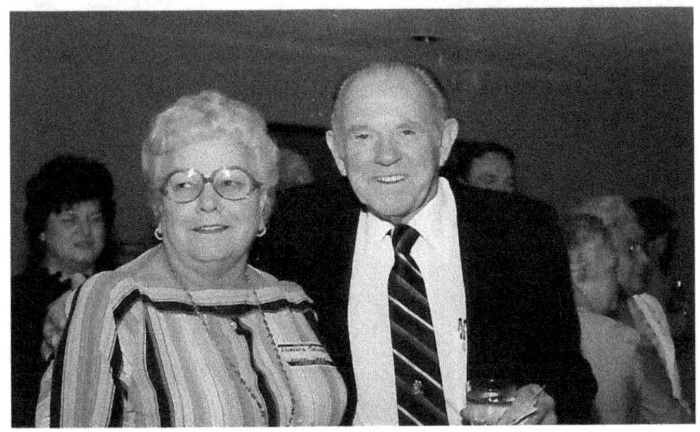

The "Host and Hostess with the Mostest," Frank and Florence Calvert. *Courtesy the Calvert family.*

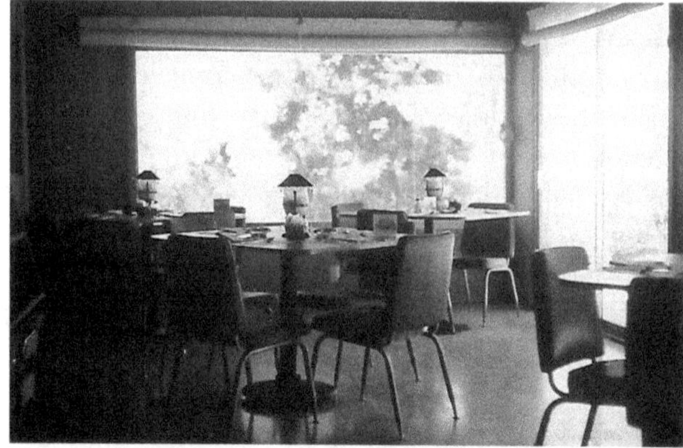

*Left*: Saguaro Corner's large picture windows give diners a glimpse at desert animals. *Courtesy the Calvert family*.

*Below*: The bar at Saguaro Corners. *Courtesy the Calvert family*.

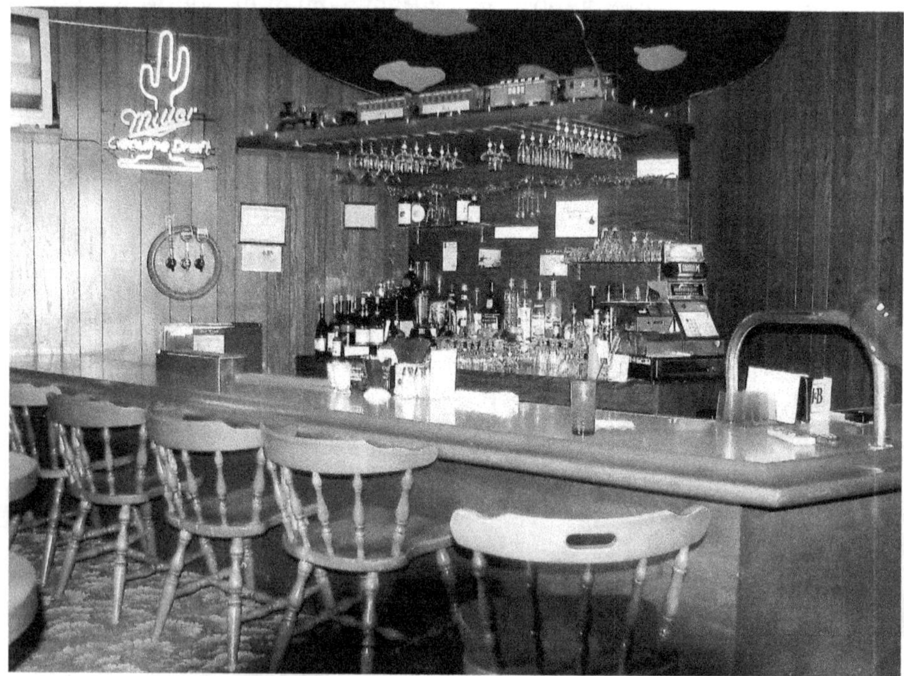


Saguaro Corners had grown from a tiny hamburger stand (and the last place to get gas before heading into the national monument) into a beautiful dining experience.

On the night that Bob returned to Tucson after his discharge, he was put to work in the kitchen because Frank had the flu. Bob worked in the kitchen until 2008. Florence's health weakened, and she died in 1995. Frank retired, but on most days he could be found at the restaurant, doing something or another. He only slowed down after a fall in 2007 when he broke a hip. A month later, he died of a heart attack at home after a day at the restaurant.

The family decided to close Saguaro Corners with hopes to eventually sell the place. In 2008, Jim Campbell, a local developer, bought the land with plans of building a resort across from the monument. "We had to buy the restaurant in order to get the option on the land," Campbell said in a phone interview. Sadly, the market tanked shortly after, and Campbell was left with the restaurant.

His idea for the restaurant was inspired by the icehouses in Texas, local places where the beer was cold and the company friendly. It was to be the seasonal counterpoint to his other restaurant, the Sawmill Run, located on Mount Lemmon. The place was in disrepair, and Campbell added about $450,000 worth of work. He created a new kitchen from one of the dining rooms, tore down areas and added a patio while trying to preserve the historical parts.

He tried a variety of ideas, but nothing worked until he hired Kade Mislinski. Mislinski had years of experience in Tucson restaurants, having worked for Sam Fox (Tucson's restaurateur of note) and opened venues in downtown just as the area was beginning to boom.

Mislinski updated the menu, modernized the space and added a craft beer program while maintaining an "emotional connection" between the restaurant and the desert. The menu today reflects modern tastes. Dave Musso, general manager and co-owner, said, "Saguaro Corners has been a place for park visitors and the locals for sixty-one years. We've upped our game." But, he added, "we're a low-key neighborhood place where people will have a great place to go for many, many years."

This is, basically, the same philosophy Frank Calvert established when he created Saguaro Corners decades earlier.

## The Best 23 Miles of Mexican Food

In August 2016, Mayor Jonathan Rothschild declared Tucson to be the home of "The Best 23 Miles of Mexican Food." Created and promoted by VisitTucson, the local visitors' bureau and a tour guide company, the loosely outlined area highlights the many Mexican restaurants found all over the city. Some are relatively new, but the ones listed below are historic and are deeply rooted in Tucson's culinary and cultural history.

### Anita St. Market (1984)

Granted this is a neighborhood market, but the lines that often reach out the door are mainly here for the fresh tortillas, burros, tacos, quesadillas, caramelos, tamales and more. Their house-made empanadas come in apple, pumpkin, pineapple, cherry and more.

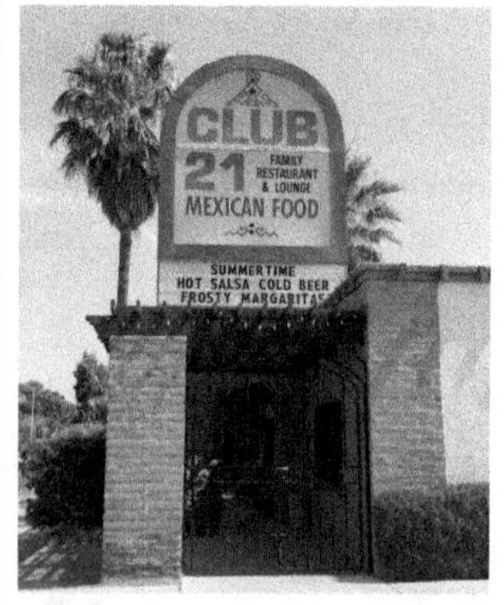


Club 21. Just how the restaurant got its name is a family legend. *Author photo.*

### Club 21 (1946)

Club 21 has been a family affair since the doors first opened in 1946.

The Jacob family, immigrants from Lebanon via El Paso, opened the restaurant as a hole-in-the-wall hamburger stand, later switching to Mexican food at the suggestion of their mother, Mary.

George Jacob moved to Tucson with his father and siblings before World War II. Shortly thereafter, the family opened Tucson Public Market, where they sold produce until just after the war. The brothers decided to open a restaurant. Family legend says that the name came from combining two discarded signs they found nearby.

George worked the kitchen, thanks to his tour as a cook in the navy during the war. Everyone else worked the front of the house and the bar.

The spot was ideal, in the heart of Miracle Mile, the stretch of road home to motor courts from the 1920s through the 1950s. At one time, from the late 1950s through the 1970s, Miracle Mile was also Tucson's restaurant row. Home to a dozen or so of the finest restaurants in Tucson, Miracle Mile fell on hard times, and many restaurants closed. Club 21 is the lone holdout.

The brothers moved on to other ventures (John opened El Parador). George hung in there, adding rooms as needed. In no time, the little cabin was a multiroom, 5,200-square-foot, full-service restaurant. Recipes are still those used at the beginning, with more added as time went by.

George brought in his son Taft, who was named after his grandfather. In 2005, George died, having worked at Club 21 until the end. Taft Jr. now runs the family business with the help of his son Taft III.

## EL INDIO (1997)

If you miss El Indio while driving south on South Sixth Street, you might need to have your eyes checked. That's because a gigantic mural is painted on a wall facing the street. Here the food is delivered by *abuelas* ("grandmothers") from rolling carts. Dressed in embroidered Mexican blouses, they place the food in front of guests with a warning of "Hot plate. Hot plate."

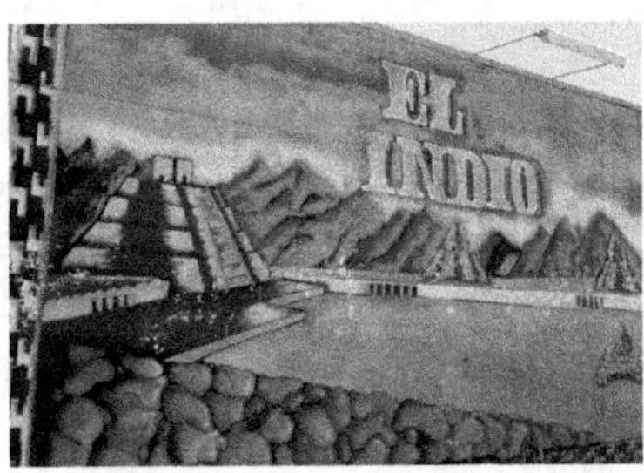


A large mural greets diners at El Indio. *Author photo.*

## EL MERENDERO (1986)

Carved out of a former drive-in, El Merendero is located on South Twelfth Avenue, another Mexican restaurant row. Seafood choices are a highlight, especially any seafood cocktails. Serving breakfast, lunch and dinner seven days a week, El Merendero is a local favorite.

## EL SAGUARITO (1989)

Alberto Vasquez first opened El Saguarito on the north side of Tucson in what was once a Taco Bell. Today, the restaurant is located more midtown and lives in the former home of a Burger King. The claim to fame here is healthy Mexican food. Vasquez used canola oil for cooking long before it was a household term. Some might wonder if the flavors get lost in translation, but with a huge following, the answer is a resounding "no."

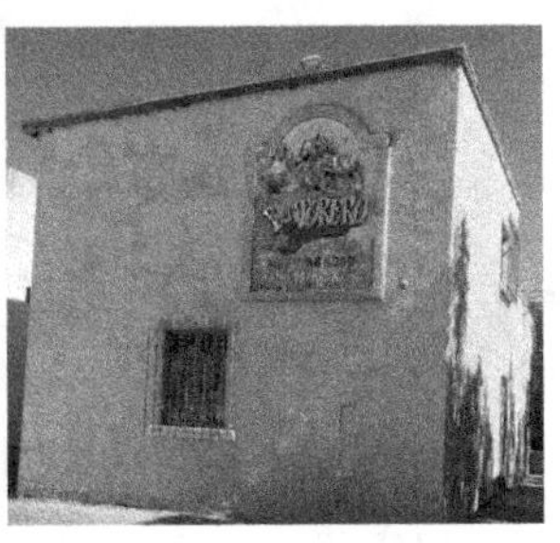

El Torero. The first Mexican restaurant that the author ever ate at after her move to Tucson. *Author photo.*

## EL TORERO (1956)

Originally located downtown, owners Adelina Borgero and Amelia Hendricks moved El Torero to South Tucson in 1958. The high-ceilinged room features a vintage bar and Mexican knickknacks. A large stuffed swordfish dominates one wall. Today, Adelina's nephew Brad Hultquist runs El Torero and still serves many of his aunt's dishes, including almendrado, a gelatin dessert in the colors of the Mexican flag.

## Guillermo's Double LL (1948)

Guillermo's Double LL restaurant stands out on South Fourth Avenue with its artfully painted exterior and huge parking lot. Not bad for a place that started out as a tiny drive-in across the street.

Don Leonard was the original owner, selling barbecue and burgers. A partnership with a man who is only known by his last name, Lawyer (the other "L"), was short-lived. In 1952, Leonard moved across the street and added Mexican food. He also brought on his son-in-law Bill Ford as partner. The drive-in disappeared in 1963, and the building expanded twice. In the 1980s, Bill added his mark to the restaurant by adding the Spanish form of his name, Guillermo.

Bill and his son Tom owned and operated the restaurant until 2008, when they sold it to a neighbor, Antonio Gonzalez, the former owner of Crossroads Drive-In, located several blocks south.

The interior is as brightly decorated as the exterior. Seafood is a specialty. Sonoran dishes are varied and plentiful.

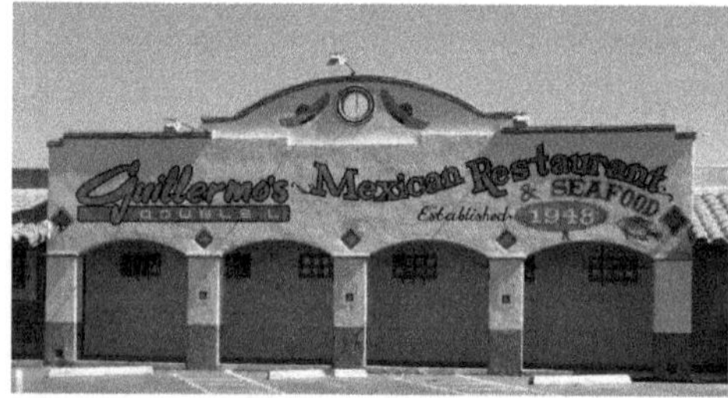


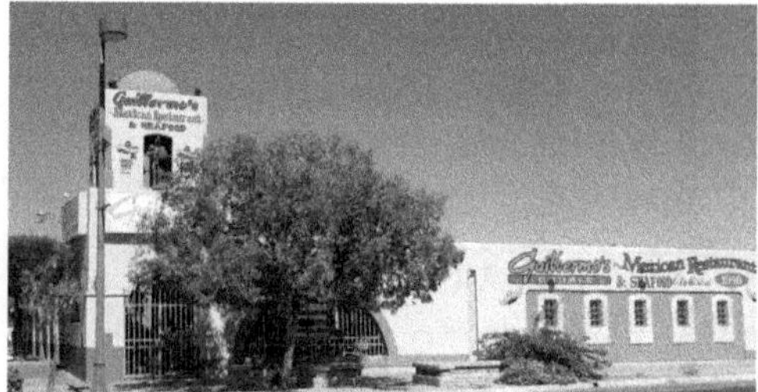

*Left*: The exterior of Guillermo's Double LL is a work of art. *Right*: Guillermo's Double LL from the street. *Author photos.*

## Rosa's Mexican Food (1970)

Rosa's first opened on Speedway Boulevard near the university and was a favorite of the college crowd. Rosa Ortega did everything, including keeping an eye on her small children. La Bandera—sour cream enchiladas with red, green and white sauces—was the specialty of the house. The kids moved the restaurant a bit farther north, and the crowd followed. Rosa's grandchildren keep the tradition going.

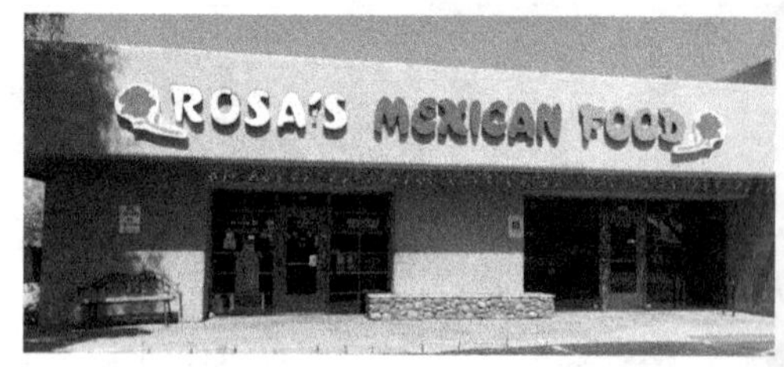


Rosa's grandchildren are making their nana's recipes, just like she did years ago. *Author photo.*

## ST. MARY'S MEXICAN FOOD (1970)

Most people in town call this west-side hole-in-the-wall St. Mary's Tortilla Factory, because the reason they go there is for the humongous flour tortillas, made fresh daily. Smaller tortillas are also available, as are fillings like carne seca, red and green chile and refried beans. Customers can take home a big family dinner. Others prefer to dine in at one of the five tables filling the tiny room. Visitors have been known to buy several dozen tortillas to take home.

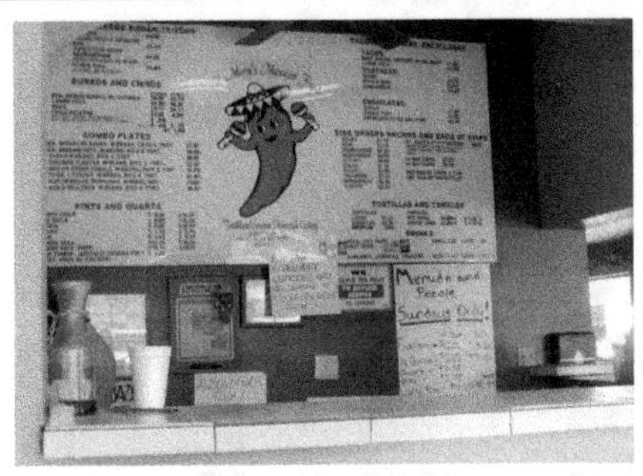

St. Mary's offers a carne seca by the pound. *Author photo.*

## TANIA'S 33 DOS MUNDOS (1981)

Located just around the corner from St. Mary's, Tania's is another restaurant as famous for its tortillas as for its food. The burros come in three sizes: regular, large and extra large. Build your own from a long list of fillings that includes red chile, green chile, beans, rice, eggs, chicken prepared several ways, calabacitas and quite a few vegan options. The soup selections are also numerous.

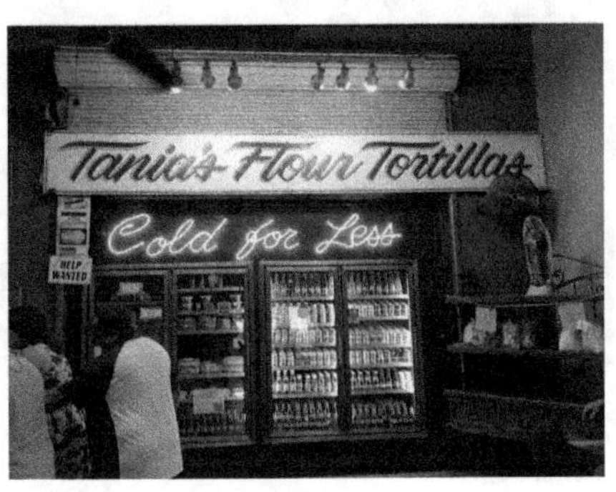


The sign at Tania's 33 says it all. *Author photo.*

## TAQUERIA PICO DE GALLO (1991)

It's small, with barely a dozen tables, but the food made here is big in flavors. The menu has many family recipes, but most folks opt for tacos. The small corn tortillas are prepared to order and come off the grill piping hot. Tortillas can be filled with the usual items—pescado (fish), carne asada (grilled beef), cabeza (head meat) or lengua (tongue). Owner Ignacio Delgado can boast that his tiny place has been featured on several Food Channel programs.

## TERESA'S MOSAIC CAFÉ (1984)

Teresa's offers some great city views, but the real show is watching tortillas being made on the flat-top grill in the middle of the busy dining room. Teresa Matias hails from a small town in Oaxaca, Mexico, and many of her dishes are done estilo de Oaxaca, including chicken mole (featured on the Food Network). Her son David, who was trained at the Culinary Institute of America, beat Bobby Flay on his *Throwdown!* show with the house huevos rancheros, a breakfast dish that can be enjoyed any time of the day.

Other historic Mexican restaurants are
Karichimaka (1949),
La Parilla Suisa (1969),
Micha's (1976),
La Estrella Bakery (1986),
Leo's (1989),
Alejandro's (1991) and
Little Mexico (1993).

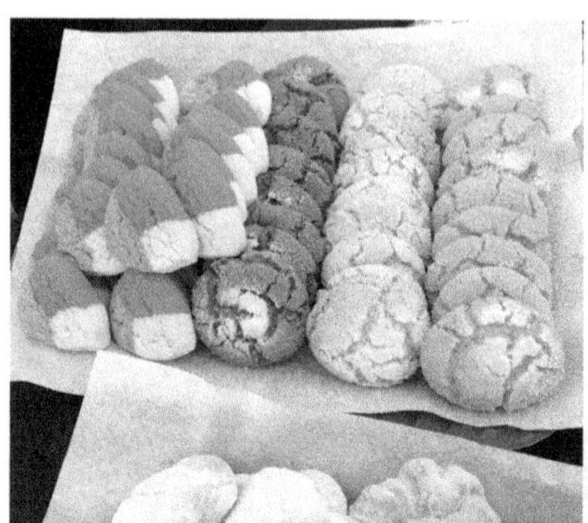

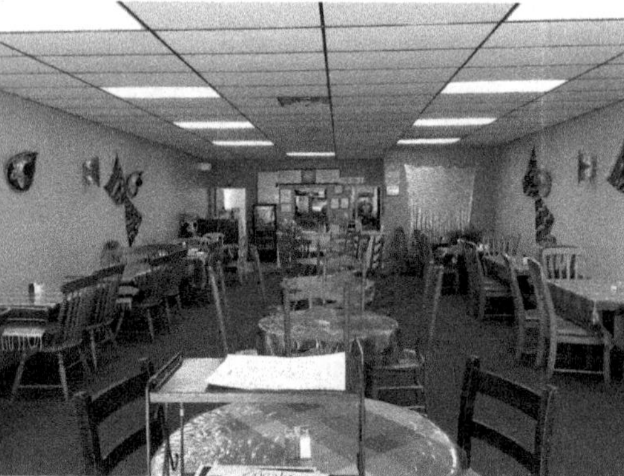

*Left*: Pan dulce from La Estrella Bakery. *Right*: Alejandro's is a downtown Tucson secret. *Author photos.*

4

# *The Times and Tastes Were A-changin'*

## *1960s–1970s*

## 1960s

### *Population: Tucson, 212,892; Pima County, 265,660*

The *Arizona Daily Star* has a series of "Then and Now" photos of Tucson on its website, Tucson.com. The pages dedicated to the 1960s tell an incredible story of rapid change under the guise of improving the city's image.

The city leaders wanted to make downtown a destination for tourists and locals. Part of the plan was to build a community center that would host major music events, conventions, festivals and more. The only way they could achieve this end was to tear down all the older structures—and that's what they did. Small businesses, theaters, grocery stores and, sadly, homes—most occupied by minority families—were destroyed. Mexican, African American and Chinese families were uprooted against their will. Controversy over the means and methods of the upheaval still rages today. There isn't enough space in this book to detail everything. The actions had a major impact on hundreds of people's lives. Although the Tucson Convention Center was completed in the 1970s, the goals laid out in the original plans were never completely met.

Another event that affected downtown's economy was the opening of El Con Mall on Broadway Boulevard. People could shop in the cool comfort of shiny new stores. The downtown department stores eventually moved to the mall, negatively affecting all the tiny businesses, especially restaurants, relying on shoppers.

But the 1960s were not all gloom and doom. After all, Tucson now had a brand-new mall. Copper, one of Arizona's economic mainstays, was hot. As in the previous decade, people were moving to the area in greater numbers. Tourism was as big as ever. Teens had cars and cruised the main drags, Speedway Boulevard and Twenty-Second Street.

In 1963, the National Association for the Advancement of Colored People organized a protest outside the Pickwick Inn, on the south side, protesting the restaurant's practice of racial discrimination. The next day, the city passed an ordinance ending, on paper at least, the right to refuse anyone service based on race or ethnicity.

In 1965, Arizona's only Five Star, Four Diamond fine-dining restaurant, the Tack Room, opened. Other restaurants that defined the decade also opened, including Gordo's Mexicateria and Mexicatessen (1963), the Iron Mask (1965) and the Palomino (1968). These are all closed now.

## PINNACLE PEAK (1962)
### FROM AN INTERVIEW WITH DAN BATES AND CASEY WILLS

The stories of Trail Dust Town and Pinnacle Peak are intertwined like old sagebrush. One is a cowboy steakhouse, the other a trip to the Old West but with fun shopping.

Trail Dust town was built in 1951 as a set for a Glenn Ford movie. In 1960, W. Howard Hamm bought the site, creating the original Trail Dust Town. At one point, it served as a starting point for a mule train that brought supplies to workers on Mount Lemmon. In the mid-1960s, one of the watering holes located in the center was bombed as part of a mob war.

Around that time, Pinnacle Peak was purchased by Mary and Bob Bates and two partners, one of whom owned Pinnacle Peak in Scottsdale. The connection was eventually dissolved, and the Bates family became sole owners of the restaurant. Today, their son Dan runs the company the Agro Land & Cattle Company.

"The early Pinnacle Peak was something to behold," said Dan Bates. The fact that it was far from town on a dirt road and had no neighbors within shouting distance added to the atmosphere. There were only two steaks on the menu: a cowgirl steak ($2.95) and the pound-larger cowboy steak ($3.95). Everything came with beans, bread and salad.

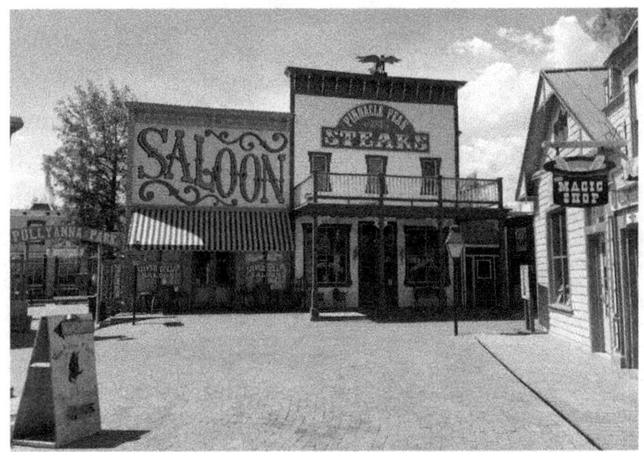


No ties allowed at Pinnacle Peak. *Author photo.*

They opted to use a cowboy staple: mesquite. This abundant local wood is hard and burns hot, perfect for cooking juicy steaks. Tables were lit by kerosene lamps. If anyone dared to wear a tie, a server cut it off and hung it on the ceiling (a practice that is still part of today's Pinnacle Peak).

Colorful stories of the early days abound. Real cowboys from nearby ranches would ride their horses to the restaurant. They'd tie their horses to the hitching posts and have a big dinner. They'd also drink several cocktails. On many nights, the staff had to toss a cowboy on his horse. Luckily, the horses knew the way home without guidance from their riders.

Then, in November 1971, tragedy struck when the whole site caught fire. Aid came from the Rural Metro Fire Department, Davis-Monthan Air Force Base and a landscaping company water truck. But with the wooden structures and all those ties, the place was a tinderbox. It burned to the ground. In less than a year, Agro rebuilt the restaurant on a different spot in "town" and took over ownership of Trail Dust Town.

Dan Bates, a renowned sculptor, is a real Western history buff. "I always wanted a Western town in the family," he said. So, armed with extensive knowledge and a small moving van, he traveled throughout the West, picking up doors, windows, lintels, finials, gingerbread trim, mirrors, lighting, tables and chairs—anything and everything he could find to make the town and restaurant authentic.

In the basement of the Goldfield Hotel in Goldfield, Colorado, he found the hotel's original bar and shipped it to Tucson. The doors of the Savoy Opera House, one of the buildings on the property, came from the royal entrance to the Savoy Hotel in London.

With the purchase of Trail Dust Town, Agro inherited two colorful characters who are as much a part of the story as the cut-off ties. One,

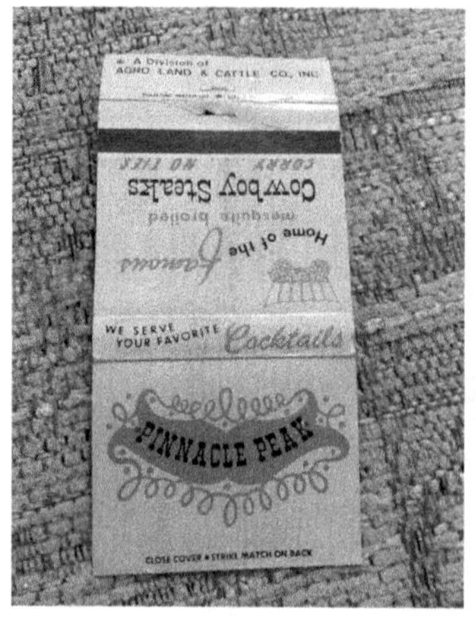


Matchbook from Pinnacle Peak. *From the collection of Gerald Gay.*

"Mr. Jack" Larrington, was bartender and manager until he retired in the 1980s.

The other was Tombstone Slim, a real cowboy who was the official marshal of Trail Dust Town. He acted as security but was also in many ways the face of Pinnacle Peak and Trail Dust Town. He wore full marshal gear, including an always-loaded .44 and a badge. He sported a scraggly beard and long hair. He was tall and imposing—even without his pistols. Kids loved him. Slim even lived on the property for a while. Today, portraits of both men hang in the restaurant as a tribute.

As the customer base grew, it was necessary to add more rooms. The Wagon Wheel Room, so named because of the lighting made of wagon wheels, is a favorite with diners. The Living Room is another dining space. To add to the Old West theme, servers take on names of famous Western characters. You can have your dinner served by Wild Bill or Belle Starr.

One thing Bates discovered in his research was that, unlike those portrayed in movie Westerns, the buildings in old Western towns were painted in bright colors, not grays and browns. So, the buildings in Trail Dust Town were painted in an array of beautiful colors. The buildings house a variety of shops. You can shop at the general store, chocolate shop, magic shop or the trading company. You can dress up in antique clothing and have a sepia-colored photo taken. Or you can have a manicure.

Located just off the courtyard is the Museum of the Horse Soldier, a historic tribute to military horsemen. Kids can ride a carousel, the Ferris wheel or the train that circles the property. And then there are the Pinnacle Peak Pistoleros, whose Wild West Stunt Show entertains guests Wednesday through Sunday evenings. What began as mock gunfights among the bussers and other staff has grown into a nationally recognized stunt show.

The food is still the draw. These days, the menu has expanded to include a big cowboy steak, brisket and barbecue from the pit grill, baby back ribs, chicken, salmon, other steak cuts, salads and even a veggie burger. Sides are more than beans. You can get a baked potato, sweet potato, corn on the cob and mixed veggies, to name a few. The fruit cobbler remains a favorite for dessert.

The tiny little cowboy restaurant has grown into an entertainment and dining destination. But Dan Bates believes there is something more. "The thing that makes Pinnacle Peak and Trail Dust Town special is the fact that we are remembering and promoting history."

And, indeed, despite all the traffic, shops and businesses surrounding it, if you squint just a little and let yourself go, you get the feeling that, maybe, the Old West still lives in a tiny part of Tucson.

## GUS BALON'S (1965)
### FROM AN INTERVIEW WITH KELLI PHILLIPS

Like many Tucsonans, Gus and Kathleen (Kay) Balon moved to Tucson for a better life. Daughter Laura had allergies, and their doctor recommended moving to a warm, dry climate.

Tucson wasn't their first stop, though. With years of experience running soda fountains in drugstores, they moved to Los Alamos, New Mexico, during the time when the Manhattan Project was in full swing. Gus got clearance and began cooking for scientists who worked on the project. It was there that he learned how to make all the breads that are still baked daily at the restaurant he opened in Tucson in 1965.

Gus and Kay met in Iowa, where they both worked at a battery factory during World War II. Gus was so taken by young Kay that he would deliberately jam his machine to stop production. Everyone would have to take a break, and he would get to talk with Kay. A whirlwind romance ensued, and they were married five months later.

The Balons traveled a bit, ending up in New Mexico. Then, because Laura's allergies were still an issue, they moved to Tucson and opened Gus's Catalina Café in 1961 and the eponymous Gus Balon's in 1965. They ran both places but decided to concentrate on the eastside location, where they soon earned a reputation for quality food and friendly service.

Customers who still eat at the place regularly talk about waiting in line for an hour or more on weekend mornings. Balon's was open seven days a week from 7:00 a.m. to 9:00 p.m. Gus, Kay and daughters Donna and Laura worked both the front and back of the house.

Eventually, the Balons decided to stick with typical diner hours and serve only breakfast and lunch, although for a few months dinner service returned.

Balon's became so popular that it gained national attention. In the book *Roadfood*, writer Michael Stern noted that when you walk into Balon's,

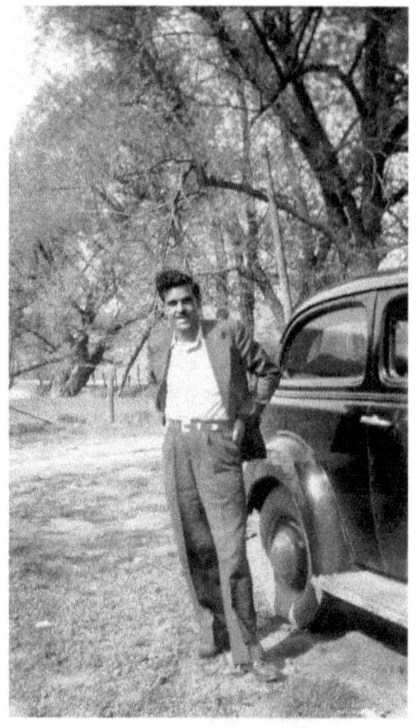

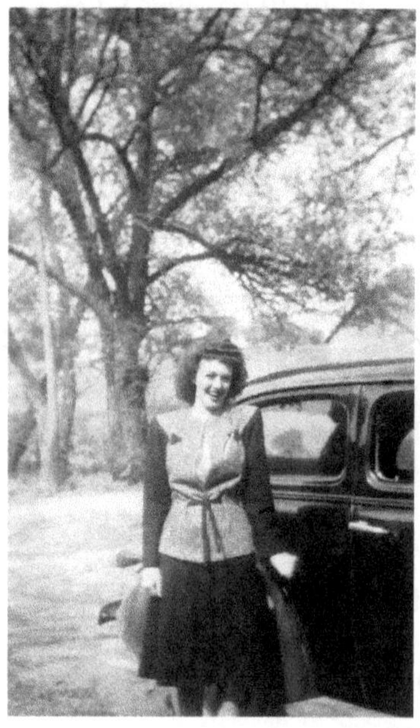

*Top*: A young Gus Balon. *Bottom*: Kay Balon prior to her move to Tucson. *Courtesy Kelli and Will Phillips*.

"your nose will tell you that this is a special place." He noted also, "The pie repertoire is staggering." And he called Balon's longtime menu staple cinnamon rolls "a scenic wonder." Epicurious.com called the giant rolls "the country's best cinnamon roll," and they even appeared in mystery writer J.A. Jance's *Queen of the Night*.

Balon's was known for all-American food at all-American prices. A full breakfast—orange juice, one egg, bacon, toast and coffee—could be had for thirty-five cents. Meatloaf and all the fixins' was eighty-five cents.

Gus retired in 1980, turning the restaurant over to Laura. But before retiring, he helped his daughter Donna and her husband, Robert Bartke, open Robert's Restaurant (see chapter 4).

Laura's children, son Chris and daughter Kelli, worked at the restaurant. Although Chris was active in the business for many years, he moved on to real estate. Kelli, on the other hand, felt the passion. When her mom and brother wanted to sell the restaurant, she said, "No!" "So, I took over the place in 2005," Kelli said. She and her husband, Will Phillips, now own and operate the restaurant in much the same way her grandparents did.

"All the recipes are the same," Kelli said. "There have probably been additions, but none of the recipes have changed. We cut our own meats. We make our own soups and gravies. We make our own pies. We come in every morning and do all those," Phillips said. Even some employees remain. Kelli noted that her current dishwasher started the year Kelli was born.

Gus died in 2007, and Kay passed away in 2016. But they are still a big part of the restaurant.

Kelli and Will wanted to honor her grandparents. On the far wall hang three large black-and-white photos of Gus and Kay. One is of Kay dressed to the nines; another shows dapper young Gus standing in front of a new car. Phillips isn't sure when those were taken, but the third was made on Gus and Kay's wedding day. They're standing in the snow, Kay looking glamourous in fur coat and heels, and Gus with his arms holding her close. This was their beginning. Although they had no idea what their future held, one gets the feeling they knew they were on to something special.

## The Cork 'N Cleaver (1966)
## From an Interview with Jonathan Landeen

Jonathan's Cork would meet the guidelines I've used for this book on its own. Owner Jonathan Landeen bought the restaurant in 1994 and has maintained a huge following since day one.

But this restaurant originally opened in 1966 as the Cork 'N Cleaver, a steakhouse chain headquartered in Phoenix. A blurb in the business section of the *Tucson Citizen* noted the groundbreaking on Tanque Verde Road for a $150,000 building that was set to be the Cork 'N Cleaver. The restaurant was going to be the first building in the modern Monaco Mall. Today, the Cork is a freestanding building with no traces of a mall.

The Cork 'N Cleaver, however, was one of the first restaurants on Tucson's future Restaurant Row, a length of road that in the 1970s would be home to the city's finest and most fun restaurants.

The Cork 'N Cleaver was known as a hip hangout with beef-centric menus, big cocktails and an atmosphere that was both intimate and convivial. In fact, the sign for the restaurant had a stylized head of a steer and, below that, the proclamation "Beef & Booze."

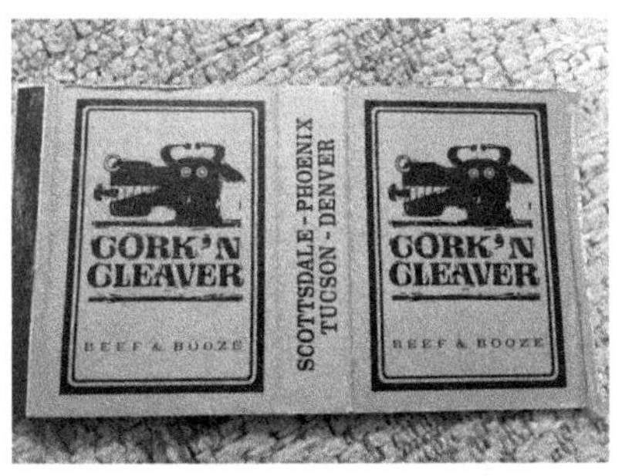


Cork 'N Cleaver matches. *From the collection of Gerald Gay.*

People fondly remember the menus that were etched into real meat cleavers. The salad bar overflowed with a vast assortment of options served on chilled pewter plates. All the dressings were made in-house; the sweet peppercorn

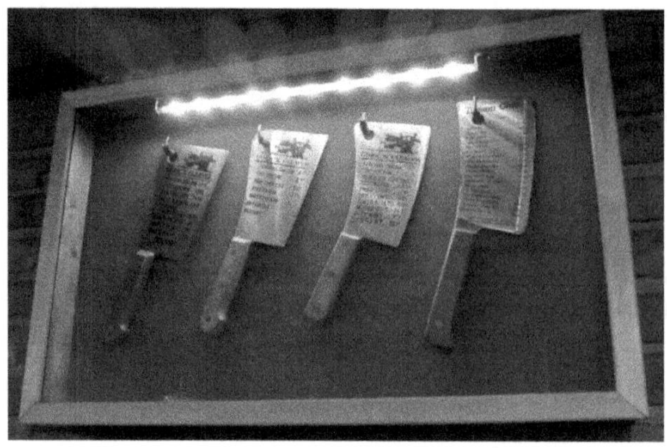

Yes, the menus were written on real meat cleavers at the Cork 'N Cleaver. *Courtesy Jonathan's Cork.*

was a favorite. A full lineup of steaks, crab legs and shrimp was on the menu. People still talk about the Cork's Pride, a twelve-ounce top sirloin marinated in teriyaki sauce and grilled. It was called "the thickest steak you've ever seen."

The space was divided into several small dining rooms, some with working beehive fireplaces. Adobe walls were adorned with bridles, bits and spurs, lending the restaurant a southwestern vibe. Dining here was intimate, cozy, warm, romantic and a haven for meat lovers. Servers, dressed in white shirts and madras shorts, treated patrons with utmost care. The list of regulars was long, and everyone seemed to know one another. Out-of-towners were given a warm welcome and made to feel like they belonged. The restaurant was so popular that the owners converted the front porch into another room and extended the bar area to accommodate diners.

In 1984, Bill Hillenbrand purchased the restaurant and changed the name to the Tucson Cork. Hillenbrand had moved to Tucson in 1981 from Batesville, Indiana, where he owned Hillenbrand Industries, a Fortune 500 company.

Hillenbrand and his wife, Doby (Dolores), adapted to their new home with gusto. The Hillenbrands became patrons of the University of Arizona and were instrumental in building an aquatic center, the women's softball field, classrooms and meeting rooms for the athletic department, new dugouts for the men's baseball field and an auditorium. People credit Bill Hillenbrand for taking the UA athletic program to a whole new level. Today, both the aquatic center and the softball field bear their patrons' name.

In spite of his wealth, Hillenbrand was a "bass-fishing, pistol-shooting, bicycle-riding former army MP...more of a $1.85 six-pack guy," according to Greg Hansen, sportswriter for the *Arizona Daily Star*. In other words, he was an ideal owner for a casual but classy place like the Cork. Hillenbrand didn't change much. He added some items to the menu, including bison, which might have been influenced by his brother's bison farm in the Midwest. Those additions meant bigger cleavers. He took down some of the tack and hung reproductions of Native American works. A writer from the *Chicago Tribune* welcomed Hillenbrand's ownership, noting that the Cork 'N Cleaver had become "an 'in' place for the yuppie crowd."

In a town loaded with steakhouses, the Tucson Cork stood out under the aegis of Bill and Doby Hillenbrand. Their association with the university brought alums, faculty and students and their families. Regular customers continued to come. New customers became regulars. But by the time Landeen and his wife, Colette, took charge, business had slowed.

Landeen had worked in New Orleans under the guidance of Paul Prudhomme and for a decade at the neighboring Solarium. Both NOLA and the Solarium had instilled in him a deep love and knowledge of fresh seafood, and so Landeen added several items to the menu. But he knew the regulars might balk. "When I bought the restaurant, I did a two-part menu. We kept what we called 'The Cork Traditions.' Those were the items that people came to eat all the time."

He eliminated the salad bar for a number of reasons, one being that it just wasn't practical for either the diner or the kitchen. Plus, it took up too much space. He respected its popularity, though, and put on the menu a salad called the "Salad Bar Salad" with all the items diners had enjoyed at the salad bar.

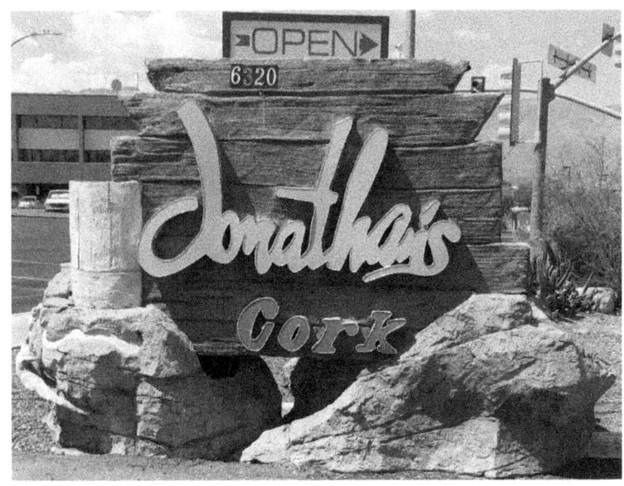


Jonathan's Cork carries on the tradition of the Cork 'N Cleaver. *Author photo.*

Landeen knew what the newer diners wanted and so, in addition to the three fresh fish options, he added ostrich, venison and other game. He expanded the beer and wine list, as customers were becoming savvier when it came to potent potables.

The building was in pretty good shape thanks to Hillenbrand's meticulous care, but Landeen added a patio on the east side of the building. Misters in the summer, heaters in the winter and outstanding views of the Catalina Mountains to the north made dining here a dream.

On most nights, Landeen works his way through the dining room, talking with guests and ensuring that they are having a great time and that the food is just right. Landeen's personality is part of the reason the restaurant is filled even in the dead of summer. With his booming voice, bushy moustache and huge smile, he's hard to miss. People love him. Colette takes a more laid-back approach and is in charge of the business end.

Tanque Verde may no longer be the hot spot it once was, but Jonathan's Cork is still where Tucsonans head when they want a memorable evening of great food, well-built cocktails and excellent service.

## LOTUS GARDEN (1968)
## FROM AN INTERVIEW WITH DARRYL WONG

"My father was the American dream," said Darryl Wong, owner of Lotus Garden, Tucson's only Chinese restaurant continuously run by the same family. "When he came here [sometime in the 1950s], he had no nickels to rub together."

Thomas Wong came to Tucson on the promise of running a market (now Anita Street Market) that was owned by an elderly relative who wanted to retire. He paid them rent as well as using sweat equity to buy the business. He worked all day, every day, paying off the debt in three years.

Then Thomas decided it was time to get married. Through some friends, he was introduced to Lillian, who lived in Detroit.

The Wongs worked the store for several years, but by then there were three children and fierce competition from convenience stores. At about the same time, they heard that a barbecue restaurant was for sale. Because it was on Speedway Boulevard near Wilmot Road—where the pavement literally ended—the price fit their budget. The Wongs opened Lotus Garden in 1968.

Darryl noted that his parents' business was the second to get a loan from the newly minted Small Business Administration. And, he added, "They were the first to pay it off." He recalled the photo taken at the bank when his dad handed over the final check.

Chinese chefs were hard to come by at the time. They tended to stay in bigger cities to be close to their families. Lotus Garden's first chef, a bachelor with no attachments, had worked in big American kitchens, so the first menu had as many American dishes as Chinese ones.

Due to the location, business was slow. One night, Thomas watched the scarce traffic on Speedway Boulevard and wondered what he could do. His brother, who was working for him, told Thomas he had the answer. A well, left over from the barbecue restaurant, sat in front of the restaurant. His brother told him that business was slow because the well was empty. Thomas filled the well with water. That week ended up being the busiest week yet. Darryl called it feng shui.

Darryl began working full time after he graduated college and today manages all of the elements customers don't see. His brother Dan is also involved in the restaurant, showing up after his work as a computer programmer at IBM.

Thomas died in 2013, but Lillian, eighty-four, still works, although not full time.

The restaurant has gone through changes over the decades: upgrades in the dining room and patio in 1985; a wine and gift shop added in 1997; and a kitchen remodel in 2009. The menu changed as well. When Lotus Garden first opened, the food was strictly Cantonese. In the early 1970s, when President Nixon opened the doors to American travel to China, people returned with a taste for fiery Szechuan cooking, so the Wongs added that style to the menu. Just about everything on the menu is made to order, so customers can get dishes prepared the way they want it. "A good owner solicits comments," said Darryl, adding that he appreciates the fact that customers will tell him what they like or don't like.

As to the success of Lotus Garden, Wong says, "Trust is the key thing. The trust that you give your customers when they come in that they're always going to get that same quality and that same flavor again and again."

In 2018, Lotus Garden celebrated fifty years in business. Since Darryl has no children, the restaurant will last as long as he and his brother can do the work. Tucsonans needn't worry—there's still a lot of feng shui energy at Lotus Garden to keep it going for some time to come.

## HISTORIC FOURTH AVENUE

"The Ave" has a happening vibe, plenty of one-of-a-kind shopping and a plethora of restaurants, many of which fit the definition of historic. Located west of the university and just north of central downtown, a trip to Fourth Avenue is easy and fun. The Sun Link Modern Streetcar runs the entire length from University Boulevard to Ninth Street.

### ATHEN'S ON 4TH (1993)

Chef and owner Anderas Delfarkas came to Tucson from Greece via Montreal, Los Angeles and a host of other cities. Serving traditional Greek fare, it may be the only white tablecloth restaurant on Fourth Avenue.

### BISONWITCHES (1998)

Known for big sandwiches, bread bowl soups and cold beer, this casual spot often has a line out the door.

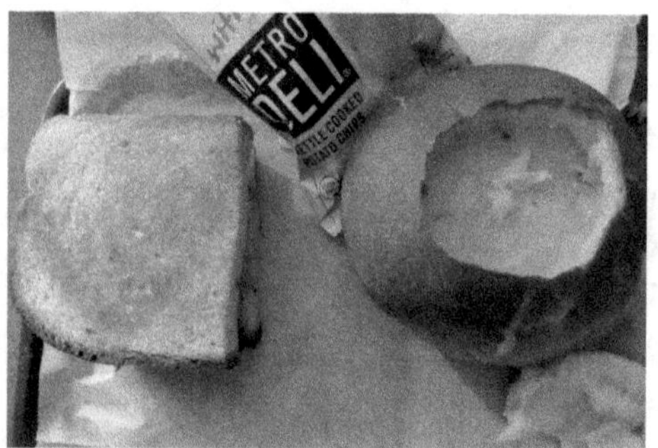


Bread bowl soup and sandwich at BisonWitches on historic Fourth Avenue. *Author photo.*

### BROOKLYN PIZZA (1996)

Whether ordering a slice or a whole pie, you can watch your pizza being prepared in the open kitchen. This may be the only pizza parlor in the United States powered by solar energy.

### CARUSO'S (1956)

See chapter 3.

### CHOCOLATE IGUANA (1989)

This is more than just a candy store. Customers can order coffees, teas and baked goods all day long. The patio is a great place for people watching.

### DAIRY QUEEN (1952)

Although originally located across the street, this is Arizona's first Dairy Queen.

### EPIC CAFÉ (1994)

The coffee house claims to be one of the oldest establishments on the Avenue. That may very well be true. Epic was serving upscale coffee and homemade eats long before those corporate places were ever conceived.

### LA INDITA (1983)

See chapter 5.

### MAGPIE'S PIZZA (1987)

The original gourmet pizza parlor in town, Magpie's set Tucson on its culinary ear when it opened. There are two other stores, but this is the original.

The following are not restaurants, but they've played a big part in the social history of Fourth Avenue.

### THE BUFFET (1929)

The only food served here are pickled hot dogs, but they are historic.

### TIME MARKET (1919)

Back in the day, this place was a little neighborhood market complete with a butcher. At one time, it was called the Pioneer Market. The market remains, but today there is a bakery/restaurant that serves great pizza hot out of the wood-burning oven.

### THE FOOD CO-OP (1972)

What began as a small group of people looking for alternative food sources has morphed into a large grocery store with a creative food menu.

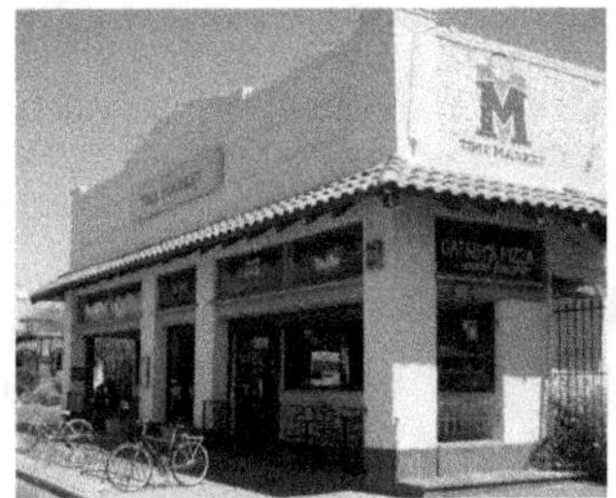


The Time Market has been transformed into an upscale market with some of the best pizza in town. *Author photo.*

# 1970s

## *Population: Tucson, 262,933; Pima County, 351,667*

The 1970s saw enormous growth in Tucson. At the beginning of the decade, the population in Pima County hovered around 350,000. By the 1980 census, the number of people living in the area was more than 530,000.

As the war in Vietnam raged, the stop-the-war movement was alive and well in Tucson, especially at the university. Beginning in the late 1960s and continuing into the '70s, the protests never reached the volume or intensity found at other universities, but there was noise.

On May 5, 1970, students occupied Old Main, the original building on campus. The takeover lasted less than a day, but the movement stayed strong until the end of the war. Other skirmishes happened between police and street people. The latter, like more monied visitors, had moved to Tucson for the weather.

The first dustups happened directly in front of the university's Main Gate. Merchants felt that the "transients" were interfering with business and called in the police. The two groups clashed when police arrested members of the group. C.L. Sonnichsen, in his book *Tucson: The Life and*

*Times of an American City*, called it a "riot." He goes on to describe how the groups then moved to Fourth Avenue, where, again, merchants were concerned about panhandling and harassment. More arrests were made. But after an organized group of street people took their case to the powers that be and merchants realized business was being affected by the bad press, police eased off. Peace was restored.

West of town at Old Tucson, films and television shows were being produced in record numbers. Films included *Death Wish* and *The Outlaw Jesse Wales*. *Gunsmoke* was filmed here for several years. *Little House on the Prairie* brought Michael Landon back to Tucson, where he became a familiar sight at restaurants, even hosting a celebrity tennis tournament in the 1980s and early '90s.

Themed restaurants seemed to be a trend. Tanque Verde Road became the new Restaurant Row. People gathered at restaurants and bars, sipping wine coolers and looking hip in their bell-bottoms and big hair. Cocaine made a brief appearance. Disco was king. And Tucsonans danced, drank and ate the night away.

## EEGEE'S (1971)
### FROM INTERVIEWS WITH ED IRVING AND DOMINICK SCALA

If someone were to make a movie about the story of eegee's, a story of the little guys who made it big, the film would be a hit with audiences, but the critics would pan it as unbelievable.

But the story is real, and the little guys—Ed Irving and Bob Greenberg—are as real as they get. They grew up together in Rhode Island. Irving had spent time at the University of Arizona. After graduation, he returned home to work for his father's company. As he and Greenberg were enjoying a couple of Italian ices, a traditional treat found all over the East Coast, and wondering what to do with their lives, they decided to take the ices to Tucson, because, "It's always hot in Tucson," said Irving.

They packed up a small moving truck and, with $1,200 each, headed west. When returning the truck to a company in Tucson, the guy at the shop asked what they were planning to do. They told him the plan was to sell frozen lemonade out of trucks, like the Good Humor man.

What followed proved to be a pattern that would be repeated throughout their career and be instrumental to the success of eegee's. People took a genuine interest in the two young men and made a point to help when

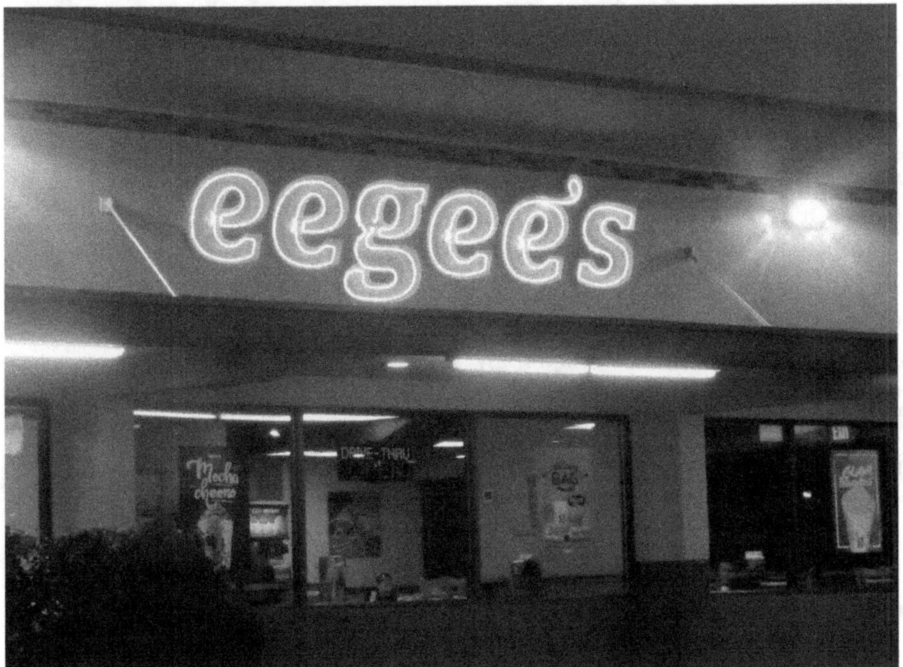


eegee's, a true Tucson original. *Author photo.*

possible. "All these people we had, I don't know if we looked inept or what," said Irving. "They would always sit us down and give us advice."

Another important piece of the pattern was the fact that Irving and Greenberg listened. In this case, the man at the truck rental store suggested they rent the small storefront across the street. It was tiny, but it fit their needs. Within weeks, they were making and selling their version of Italian ice.

They called the business eegee's, a phonetic spelling of the initials of their names. The creation wasn't quite the Italian ice they had back home. "We were missing a few details," Irving joked. Nonetheless, their creation was a hit, and they decided to take the show on the road. They bought a former postal truck for $500, outfitted it with a freezer and began selling the ices near local high schools. But they ran afoul with school officials and were forced to stop.

"We thought we were done," Irving said. Someone told them about a construction site where hundreds of new homes were being built. They listened and took the truck to the site. Every day, construction workers would line up to buy the ice-cold slushes. The hungry workers suggested that Irving and Greenberg sell sandwiches. There was an Italian deli near their store that was also home to an Italian bakery—a perfect source for the grinders they'd decided to make. Grinders, an Italian sub sandwich, were another favorite from back in Rhode Island. They made a dozen, which sold out in a matter of minutes. The next day, when they returned to the deli to buy more cold cuts, the owner asked, "What the hell are you doing with all those cold cuts?" When Greenberg and Irving explained, he said they'd never make money buying meat that way. He encouraged them to buy the food wholesale.

At the wholesaler, they met a man called Tony D'Augustino. He suggested they buy a meat slicer, and while they were at it, they should add a roast beef sandwich to the menu. To help, he gave them a whole roast beef with the idea that if the sandwich sold, they would buy beef from him. Again, the sandwiches were a hit. Turkey followed, then ham.

The trucks were retired; eegee's expanded into brick-and-mortar stores.

An early hire, Dominick Scala, would turn out to be one of the best employees. "I started working there in 1975, the summer between my junior and senior years in high school," said Scala, who worked his way up, eventually running eegee's massive commissary and contributing invaluable time and energy. Irving credits a great deal of the success of the business to Scala. He only recently left the company.

Operations were moved to a huge commissary on the south side. The move allowed them to make more items in-house: baking bread and cookies, making the dressings and sauces, slicing the meats and, of course, making the eegee's ices. Little by little, the partners would add items to the menu or change the way they did things, always heeding advice people felt compelled to share. "We both had to agree, or it didn't happen," said Irving. "It made us more thorough, because we had to make a case with each other."

In the early days, people would watch their sandwiches being made on an assembly line. In 1977, inspired by some careful research, sandwich building moved into the back, and a french fry machine was added. "French fries are where it's at," said Irving, noting that with the addition of fries, eegee's became a "real" restaurant.

Other changes came directly from the workers. "Our employees are the greatest source for new things," said Irving. An employee volunteered to make the meatballs when the ones the company bought were inconsistent. Another employee re-did the cookie recipe. The pizza pretzel went from being an employee snack to a popular menu item.

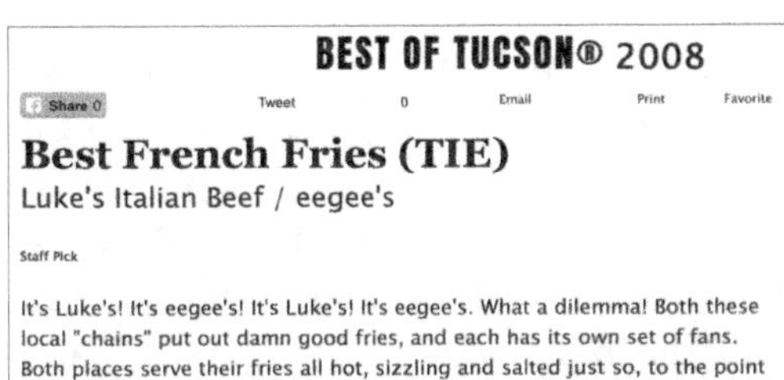

BEST OF TUCSON® 2008

Share 0 Tweet 0 Email Print Favorite

**Best French Fries (TIE)**

Luke's Italian Beef / eegee's

Staff Pick

It's Luke's! It's eegee's! It's Luke's! It's eegee's. What a dilemma! Both these local "chains" put out damn good fries, and each has its own set of fans. Both places serve their fries all hot, sizzling and salted just so, to the point that they barely need ketchup (and, *please*, no ranch dressing!). Yes, they are greasy, but in a good way. And oddly enough, the signature sandwiches (the Italian beef at Luke's and the grinder at eegee's) seem to be the perfect foil to the taters. Tucsonans should consider themselves lucky to have two hometown places serving such delicious fries.

*Left*: The author wrote this piece for *Tucson Weekly* and unknowingly saved eegee's french fries. *Below*: An eegee's grinder wouldn't be complete without fries and their famous slushy drink. *Author photos.*

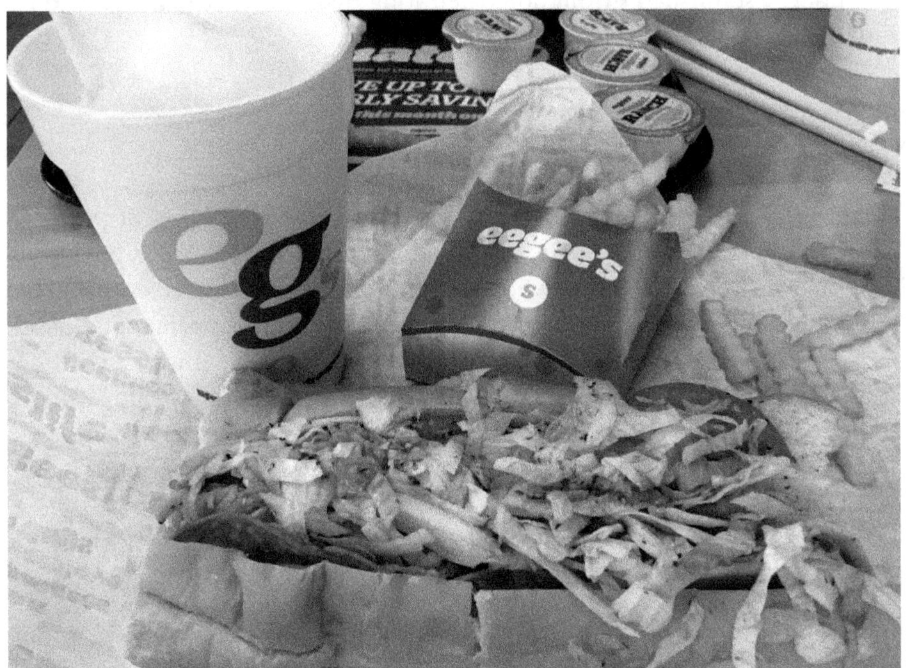


Eegee's was—and remains—big on giving back to the community. A coupon program that began in 1995 is still going strong. In the first year, $12,000 was donated to the Community Food Bank. In 2015, the program raised $300,000 for another local charity. Eegee's has a policy of never using day-old bread. Any leftover bread is delivered to the Santa Maria soup kitchen; leftover meats and vegetables are donated to homeless shelters.

Another payback was hiring people with disabilities. Beacon Foundation has been a Tucson icon when it comes to training programs for that population. Its main office was right behind a midtown eegee's. "We worked with Beacon for years," said Scala. He added that many Beacon clients have worked with the company for years. (Eegee's gives all employees bonuses for longevity every ten years.)

One blip in the operations was a failed attempt to expand to Phoenix. Irving and Scala gave several reasons why eegee's didn't make it in Phoenix, but they consider it a lesson learned the hard way. In 2006, Irving and Greenberg sold the business to CEO Foods, a family company that had owned several Jack-in-the-Box restaurants in California.

The new owners carry on the traditions that Ed Irving and Bob Greenberg established throughout their long ownership of eegee's. And to think it all started out of the back of a truck.

## GENTLE BEN'S (1971)

The original location was in an old home just off the University of Arizona campus. It was thus a popular spot for the college crowd. Years back, the location was home to another college hangout, the Yucca Tearoom. The building has also housed a couple of fraternities and a boardinghouse, and for a time it served as the residence of the president of the university.

In 1987, the original Gentle Ben's was torn down to make way for a high-rise hotel. The eatery then moved down the street on University Boulevard. Ben's eventually morphed into Gentle Ben's Brewing Company, probably the first local brewery in town.

A sister restaurant/brewery today, Barrio Brewery, has its own restaurant on the far side of downtown. Ben's remains a favorite college hangout, especially when UA is playing a big game.

## CUSHING STREET BAR & RESTAURANT (1972)

In the early 1970s, officials proposed a modern parkway that would cross Tucson from near Davis-Monthan Air Force Base to just south of downtown. The Butterfield Express Parkway would shorten the crosstown drive time. But in order to build the multilane road, major portions of the historic barrios would have to be razed.

The idea didn't sit well with a group of people who loved the old neighborhoods. They decided to purchase many of the homes and other buildings in Barrio Viejo, one of Tucson's oldest neighborhoods, as a way

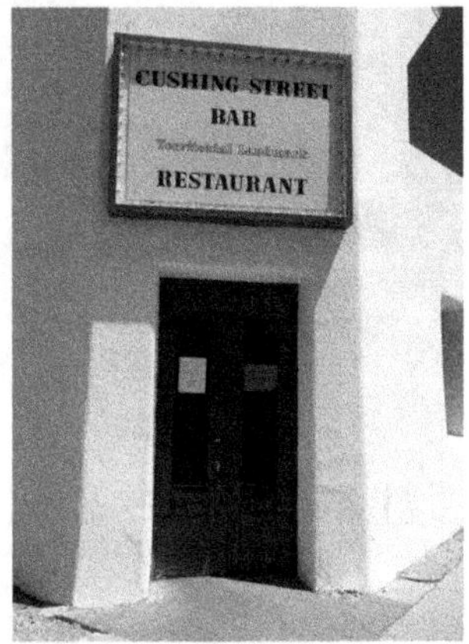


Cushing Street entrance.
*Author photo.*

to preserve them. One couple, Kelley and Sally Rollings, purchased a building on the corner of Cushing Street and Meyer Avenue. The building had been a home to the Ferrin family in the late 1800s and had also served as a store. The Rollingses planned to open a restaurant. But the place was in serious disrepair. The roof was almost nonexistent, and numerous creatures were using it for nesting.

But the Rollingses were determined, and they began restoring parts, rebuilding others and adding a room. They found antiques dating from about the time the original building was constructed. A floor-to-ceiling glass cabinet was set behind a polished wooden bar. An 1880s Steinway piano was installed to be used for live music. The pièce de résistance is the art nouveau marble statue of Cleopatra that stands in the entryway.

The Rollingses created a simple menu with good food ranging from a velvety chicken lemon soup to a Cajun meatloaf. Jazz and acoustic music were also part of the draw.

In 1989, the Rollingses sold the restaurant to concentrate on their business of restoring old homes. A handful of owners kept the restaurant open, but they all went bankrupt. The Rollingses' daughter Betsy decided she wanted to continue her parents' legacy. After a thirty-month closure and some renovations, Cushing Street Bar & Restaurant reopened 2002

Betsy Rollings kept many of the same menu items but updated the wine list. Today, diners can enjoy a nosh or a full meal after an evening at the Tucson Community Center, located across the street.

## BLUE WILLOW (1978)
### FROM INTERVIEWS WITH JANET SEIDLER AND REBECCA RAMEY

In 1978, breakfast options were limited in Tucson.

There were the chains and a handful of greasy spoon diners, but if someone wanted real food, fresh food or a breakfast made with healthful ingredients, they were out of luck.

This dearth of dining options was what inspired Janet Seidler to open the Blue Willow. At that time, Seidler owned the Unicorn Café, a tiny coffee

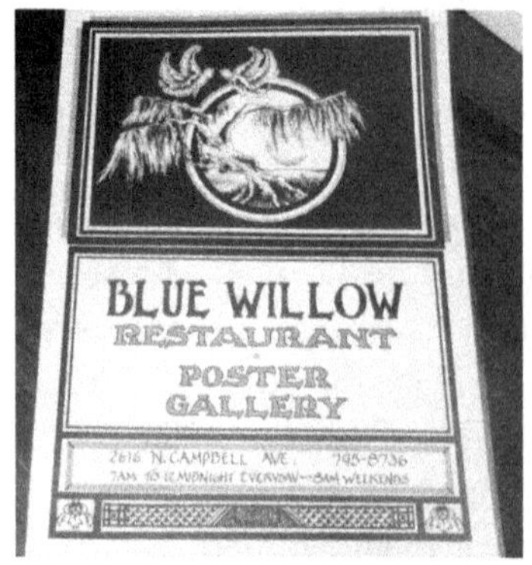


*Left*: The original menu from the Blue Willow. *Below*: The exterior of the Blue Willow. *Author photos*.

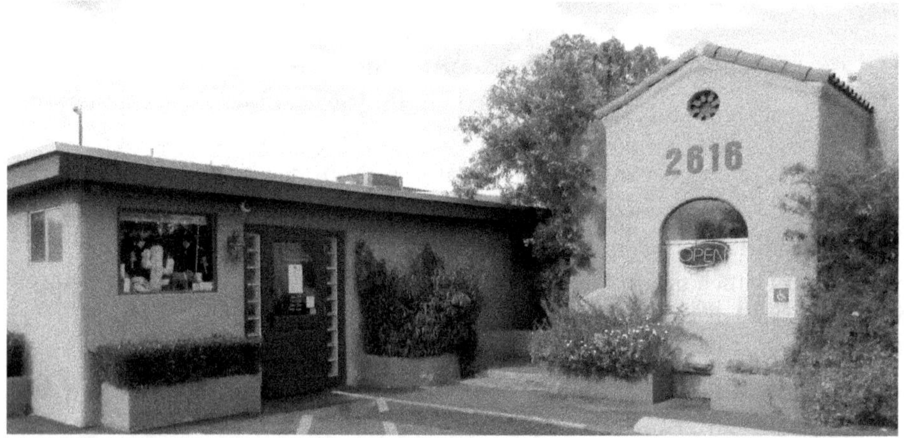


house like the ones she had enjoyed during her years in San Francisco. Despite the fact that the Unicorn was the first place Tucsonans could sip a true espresso or enjoy rich, made-from-scratch baked goods, the choices for breakfast were grim.

Seidler grew up in Tucson. When she moved to San Francisco in the early 1970s, she was blown away at the amount of fresh, healthful food she saw everywhere. She knew she could do something similar in her hometown. So, along with a friend who owned the Book Stop, a large used bookstore, Seidler decided to open her dream restaurant. They found an old adobe house on Campbell Avenue just blocks from the bookstore. Over the decades, the adobe building had previously served as a rental for university folks, a mechanic's garage, an antiques store and a daycare center. "It was a complete mess," said Seidler, "It took a while, and there was a lot of work."

They transformed the place into a charming dining spot. The tiny rooms added a certain coziness. The walls were filled with local art. There was a fireplace. Every meal was served on classic Blue Willow china. Seidler also opened a poster gallery in the front of the building, because she wanted people to have a source of great art at affordable prices.

Much of her inspiration came from her culinary hero, Julia Child. Everything was made from scratch, and most of the ingredients were local and fresh, something unheard of at the time. "People who grew vegetables and fruits would come to the back door to see if we would buy them," Seidler said.

The lovely handwritten menu offered crepes, quiche, pancakes and a full page of omelets stuffed with vegetables, cheeses, meats and more. The Blue Willow was exactly what Tucsonans were looking for, and the place became a hit.

As popular as the breakfasts were, the daily, made-from-scratch baked goods also drew hungry diners. The chocolate sour cream cake that Seidler learned to make from her mom was a top seller (and still is).

After about a year, her partner left, and Seidler eventually sold the Unicorn to concentrate on the Blue Willow. She was also the mom of two-year-old daughter Rebecca.

Dinner was served. Items included lasagna, chili (another family recipe), curry, soups, sandwiches and several vegetarian options (another concept with limited choices at the time).

In 1992, Seidler sold the restaurant to pursue other interests. Then, seven years later, due to life's twists and turns, she was back at the helm, this time with Rebecca at her side. "It took about five months to get it back on track," Seidler said. She was concerned that people wouldn't return. "But they remembered us," she noted. The Blue Willow reopened on Labor Day weekend 1999. It closed early because it was so busy, they ran out of food.

Today, Rebecca Ramey co-owns the Blue Willow. Seidler credits her with the restaurant's continuing success. "There's so much that she's done. She's done a lot of things that needed to change, like adding wi-fi," Seidler said with pride. She added that 2016 was their best year in its thirty-nine-year history.

Crowds still patiently wait for tables, but they have plenty to keep them entertained. The poster shop is now a gift shop filled with jewelry, cards, games, wind chimes, socks and quirky gift items.

Year after year, the Blue Willow wins numerous "Best of" awards in local publications—and not just for food. The patio has held the title for years running. Thanks to Ramey and Seidler, the Blue Willow will continue to be a Tucson favorite.

## ROBERT'S RESTAURANT (1978)
## FROM AN INTERVIEW WITH BOYD BARTKE

The cinnamon rolls made every day at Robert's Restaurant are an old family recipe, one that dates back to Gus Balon's restaurant on Twenty-Second Street. But this isn't a case of industrial espionage.

Robert Bartke, the original owner of Robert's, was a son-in-law of Gus Balon. When Robert opened his own place in 1978, he brought the recipe, along with others, with him.

Bartke had been a Tucson police officer and used to go to Gus Balon's on a regular basis. Whether it was for the food or to visit with Donna, Gus's daughter, doesn't really matter, because the two later married, and Bob started to work at the restaurant when Gus and his wife both developed cancer.

Robert had worked there for eleven years when he and Donna decided to open their own place. In 1978, they took over a building on the busy corner of Speedway Boulevard and Alvernon Way. The building had for many years been a Burger Chef and then, for a very short time, a German restaurant.

Logically, they named the new restaurant Robert's. The midtown location, with its warm and friendly atmosphere, and those cinnamon buns helped create a regular crowd. Robert and Donna added their own touches to the menu, but they continued the traditions established by Gus. All the breads—even the hamburger buns—and pies were made from scratch. They ground the beef for the burgers, soups and sauces in-house.

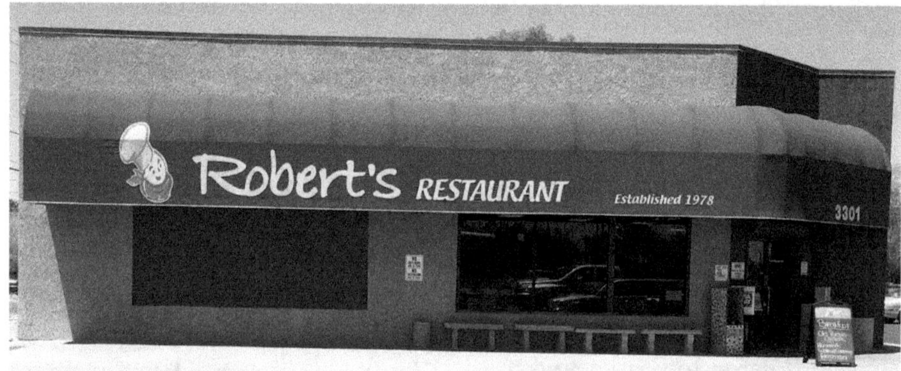


Robert's Restaurant has its roots in Gus Balon's. *Author photo.*

Then, in 1993, as it seemed to be happening everywhere in town, the city planners decided to widen Speedway Boulevard. Robert loved the atmosphere of his restaurant, but progress won, and they bought a building on Grant Road. The building once housed a major auto parts store, which meant gutting the building and basically remodeling the entire space. Boyd, Robert's son, remembers spending the summer of his senior year in high school helping the family with the major project.

Oddly, the original Balon's restaurant had been located practically across the street from Bartke's place. The new restaurant and the old place were miles apart, but the regulars followed, and the new neighbors were thrilled to have such a homey, clean diner nearby.

In 1995, Boyd began working full time at the restaurant. Robert taught his son all the tricks of the trade that his father-in-law had taught him. Boyd took over when his dad retired in 1995 and, today, runs Robert's the same way his dad, mom, grandmother and grandfather did.

Some of the staff have worked at Robert's for decades. A kitchen staffer has been there for fifteen years, and one server started the same year Boyd did (1995). Other employees claim ten or more years.

Customers come in every day, sometimes for both breakfast and lunch. They appreciate a staff that treats them like family. They like the cleanliness (one called the restaurant "a clean greasy spoon"). And they love the homemade food, ranging from simple bacon and eggs to tacos and spaghetti. Daily specials are on a regular weekly rotation, so customers know when their favorite will be served.

Boyd has added a few items, like the jalapeño bread and the Southwest eggs benedict, and the decor has been updated. A beautiful hand-drawn sign lists the pies and desserts. It sits right next to the pie case, which has been there for ages. You can buy pies by the slice or take a whole pie home. Robert's sells all the breads, too.

But those cinnamon rolls still get made twice a day, every day except Sunday, the only day Robert's closes. Robert's also closes the entire month of July so the staff can get some well-deserved rest.

5

# *If You Can't Find It Here*

## *1980s and Beyond*

## 1980s

*Population: Tucson, 330,537; Pima County, 531,443*

In the 1980s, Tucson was getting noticed by the rest of the country for something other than "being that Arizona city that isn't Phoenix." Not all of it was positive, but people still noticed.

In late September 1983, Tropical Storm Octave paid a visit. Lingering over the entire state, the storm brought a week of hard rain. In a period of thirty-six hours during the first week in October, four inches of rain fell. In most parts of the country, those numbers might not seem like a lot, but after a very wet summer and days of unending precipitation, Tucson was near drowning. The banks of the rivers collapsed, major bridges got swept away, roads were washed out and thousands of people were without power. Buildings that once held the enviable location of sitting along the rivers fell into the water. All the chaos made the national news.

In studies that followed, it was determined that decades of erosion, not the deluge itself, had caused the majority of the damage. In response, Pima County built seventy-eight miles of "soil cement bank protection" along the banks of the three rivers in the area. Eventually, parks were added. Today, hikers and bicyclists can travel the entire length of the Santa Cruz and Rillito Rivers.

Prior to the floods of 1983, the Tucson Mall had opened up on the burgeoning north side. The new mall had all the trimmings, including being totally enclosed. Shoppers headed there rather than El Con Mall, which suffered much the same fate downtown had when El Con opened a decade earlier.

Recreation became an important economic factor. In 1982, the first El Tour de Tucson was held. The bicycle race covered 101 miles around the perimeter of Tucson. In those first years, the riders were mostly locals, but every year, more and more cyclists came to "Do El Tour."

On the culinary end, Tucson was getting plenty of positive press. Café Poca Cosa had a write-up in *Gourmet* magazine; dozens of other national stories followed. Donna Nordin and her husband, Don Luria, opened up their New Southwestern restaurant, Café Terra Cotta. Nordin, too, drew the interest of the foodie press and was featured on PBS's *Great Chefs of the West* series. Janos Wilder, whose downtown restaurant, Janos, showed people back east that Tucson diners appreciated local ingredients, cooked in fine French style.

## LE RENDEZ-VOUS (1981)
## FROM AN INTERVIEW WITH GORDON BERGER

Over the decades, French restaurants in Tucson have come and gone. This is especially true when it comes to classic French restaurants. While today there are a few casual cafés, only one classic French restaurant remains: Le Rendez-vous.

First opened by Jean-Claude Berger in 1981, Le Rendez-vous is now run by his son Gordon. Gordon made some changes when he took over, but basically the menu has remained faithful to his father's vision.

The senior Berger came to Tucson from Chicago, although he'd spent a lifetime in the restaurant business in his native France. In Chicago, he worked at Maxim's and also owned his own place. In Tucson, he headed the kitchens at both Westward Look Resort and Tucson Country Club.

But when Berger heard that a lot on Fort Lowell Road was for sale, he, with the help of his parents, purchased the property and then built a restaurant, adding a small house in the back for his parents. Gordon remembers spending many nights there while his parents worked.

Le Rendez-vous was a hit from the beginning. Reviews were glowing, and awards from all major publications started pouring in on a regular basis. A

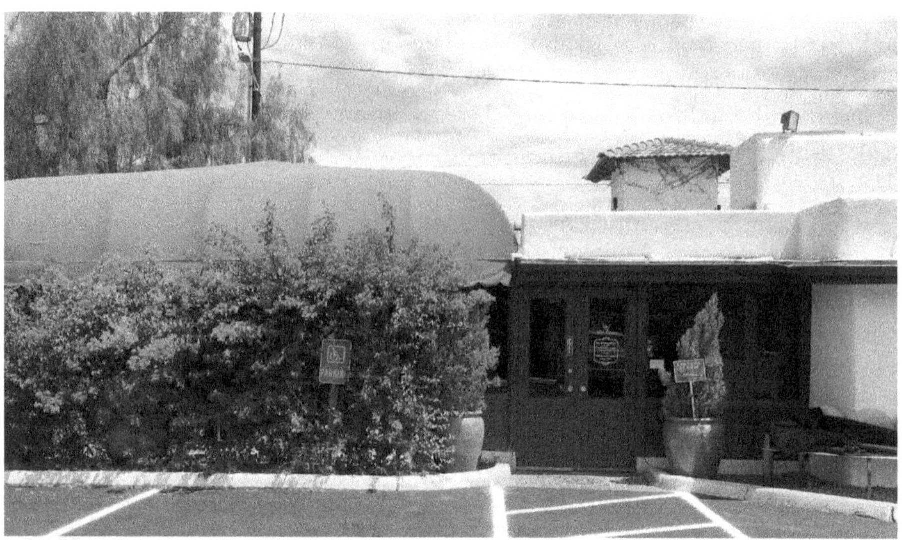

Le Rendez-vous. Tres jolie! *Author photo.*

loyal following of regulars developed. Favorite dishes were beef Wellington, salmon jalousie and duck with cherries. Customers had a choice of quality wines imported from France curated by Jean-Claude's father, Robert.

Berger had a program where he brought young chefs from France to train at the restaurant. Several went on to have their own successful—at least for a while—French restaurants in Tucson. Having well-trained kitchen staff allowed Jean-Claude to transition to the front of the house, where he assumed many roles, including sommelier, although he still maintained a hand in the kitchen.

The area around the restaurant was fairly rural when Le Rendez-vous first opened, but as the city grew, so did traffic. When Fort Lowell Road, in front of the restaurant, was widened, the restaurant underwent serious renovations. In spite of all the construction both inside and out, business at the restaurant remained steady.

As he grew, Gordon did various jobs at the restaurant. "My dad put me to work. I remember my first job was picking up nails out of the parking lot," he said. His dad brought him into the kitchen at an early age. He tells the story of when he was learning to cook fish. He tried to flip the fish and ended up splashing hot oil on himself and anyone who was within splashing distance. He decided cooking was not for him but continued working in positions from dishwasher to server. "My dad had to push me," he said.

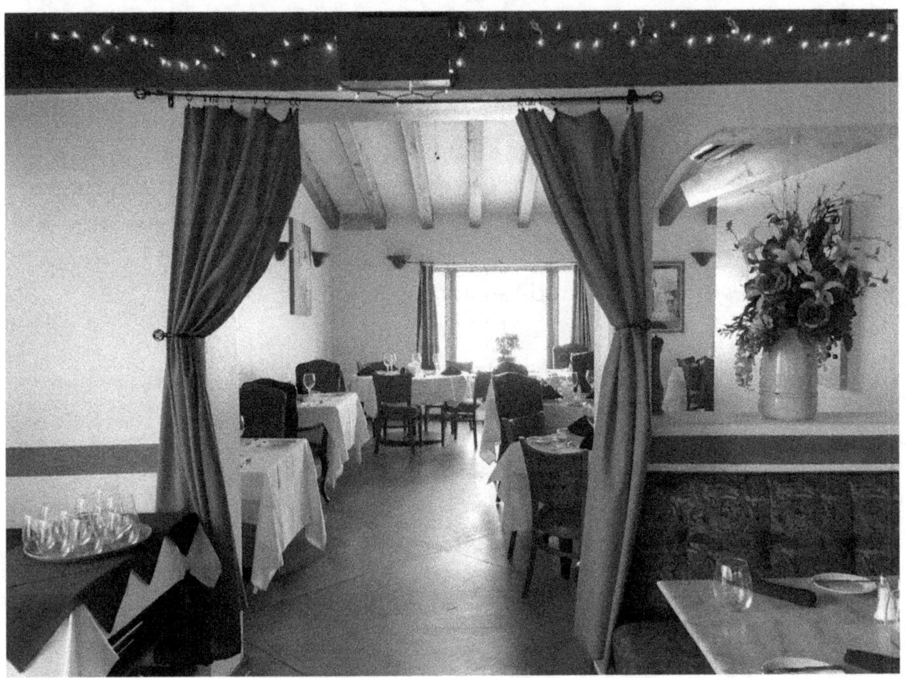

The inside at Le Rendez-vous is like a garden. *Author photo.*

The family owned a restaurant on Fourth Avenue called Café Sweetwater, which, after the Bergers divorced, was owned by Gordon's mom, Alexandria.

Gordon decided to go to the University of Arizona, graduating with a degree in math, which, he noted, would help him run the business end of the restaurant. He then decided to follow his girlfriend to France, where she was studying to be a pastry chef. She had to return to the States due to visa issues, but because he had dual citizenship, he ended up spending three years in various parts of France, working in a full range of kitchens. Even so, upon his return, he wasn't sure he was ready to take over the restaurant.

He worked for his mom at her restaurant on Fourth Avenue for a while. He tried real estate, still somewhat reluctant to get into the family business. But, like the clientele, Jean-Claude was growing older. He persuaded Gordon to take the reins. Gordon bought the restaurant from his dad and took control in 2012. Gordon had some ideas to attract a younger crowd, but now it was Jean-Claude who was reluctant. An outside consultant was hired, and both the menu and the physical layout underwent major changes.

The dining room in the back remained formal, serving the classic Le Rendez-vous menu. The front room was turned into a bistro and took on a more casual feel, resembling a garden. A small-plates menu was added. "We added a happy hour," Gordon said. Diners could come in, order several menu items and have a reasonably priced glass of wine or two without spending a longer, more formal evening.

Gordon runs the entire show these days with the help of an expert staff. But on certain evenings, Jean-Claude stops by for dinner, a glass of wine and to say hello to many of the original customers who still come to Le Rendez-vous for an elegant evening and fine dining à la française.

## La Indita (1983)

"The Little Indian Woman" was originally located downtown in the building that later became the original Café Poca Cosa (see following story). For a while in the early 1990s, there was also a location way out on East Broadway.

But La Indita settled in on Fourth Avenue, and that's where it sits today. Maria Garcia, a Tarasca Indian, was originally from Michoacán, Mexico, and spent time on the Tohono O'odham reservation. Garcia raised a family on the reservation with a very limited budget and often had to get creative with what was available to her.

Many dishes at La Indita reflect those influences and are decidedly different from your typical Sonoran dishes (although those can also be found on the menu). For example, the Tarascan taco is masa sealed around your choice of

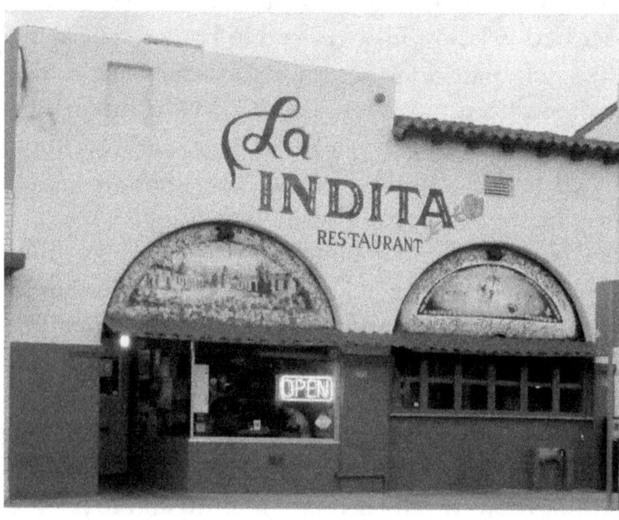


La Indita means "Little Indian Woman." *Author photo.*

filling. The Tohono O'odham taco uses a large, puffy popover instead of a tortilla. The ranch-style flat enchiladas are stacked with layers of house-made tortillas, onions, red chili sauce, oregano and cheese and then finished off with a blend of potatoes, carrots and a special sugar cane vinegar.

The front area is small, but the high ceiling gives a sense of open space. Booths line the walls. One wall is filled with a bright, colorful mural of life in a Tarascan village. There is a smaller room in the back.

Maria is retired, but her family continues the traditions "the little Indian woman" began more than thirty years ago.

## Café Poca Cosa (1984)
### From an Interview with Suzana Davila

Suzana Davila was working at an interior design studio in downtown Tucson in the 1980s. There wasn't much happening in downtown in those days. People had migrated to the new, modern malls closer to their homes and only traveled downtown to go to court or pay a bill.

Dining choices were very limited, so she often ate lunch at a tiny spot called La Indita (see previous story) on Scott Avenue. La Indita was run by Maria Garcia, a Tarasca Indian from deep in Mexico. "One day I said to her, being very brave, 'If you ever want to sell the place, I would be interested,'" said Davila. "And she looked at me and said, 'Come back and talk to me tomorrow morning.'"

Shortly thereafter, in spite of not having much money, Davila found herself the owner of that very same little spot, thanks to Garcia's generous payment plan.

Davila's father had owned a restaurant in San Carlos, Mexico, from where the family migrated when Suzana was fifteen. He was a natural partner and consultant. "My parents were always excellent cooks," she said, noting that daily trips to the market to buy dinner were the way things were done in Mexico. This method of food shopping would be a lesson that would serve Davila well as she grew her restaurant. "I wanted to bring something different," she said, referring to all the Sonoran food in town. "I wanted to bring something from all the regions of Mexico; to bring the molés, the pipians, the cochita de pibil."

Poca Cosa's name came about as they were decorating the space in preparation for opening. Her dad commented that it was such a *poca cosa*, or "little space." Davila had found the perfect name.

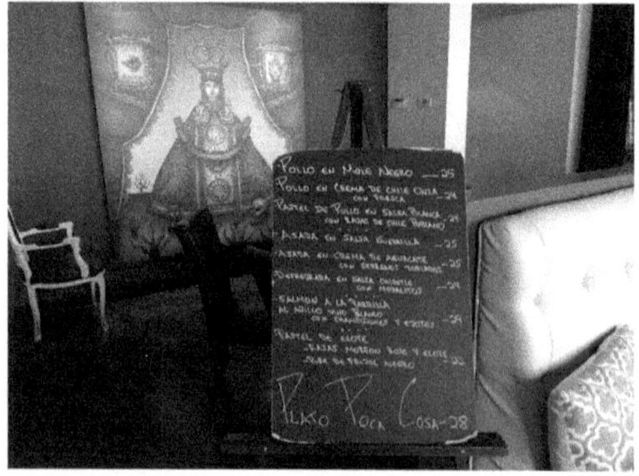

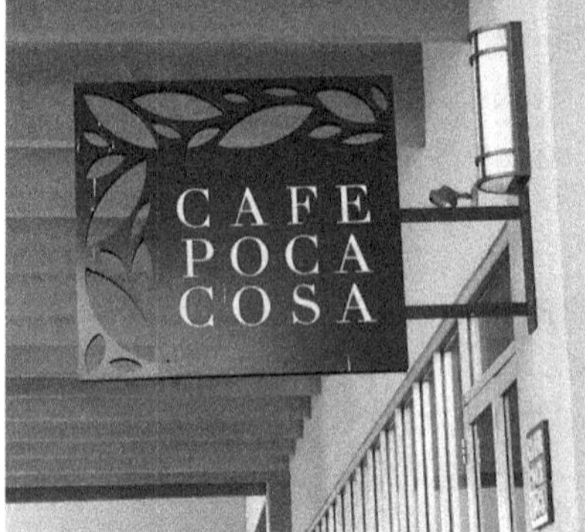


*Left*: The menu changes twice a day at Café Poca Cosa, so it is written on a chalkboard. *Right*: The sign is small; the food is big. *Author photos*.

From the beginning, Café Poca Cosa was a family affair. The chairs and tables came from her brother's furniture store. The original recipes came from her dad and mom. Various family members would sometimes work during busy hours.

She wanted her food to be as fresh as it could be. So, like her parents before her, she started going to the markets in the morning and then using the ingredients found there as inspiration for the daily menu. This was to become a trademark for Café Poca Cosa. To this date, the menu changes twice a day depending on what Davila finds at the markets.

Within weeks of the opening, the city started tearing up the old trolley tracks that ran on Scott Avenue directly in front of the restaurant. Access to the restaurant was limited by the piles of dirt that sat at the front door. Rather than bemoan the fact, Davila decided to "go around the pile of dirt to talk to the workers," she said. "I asked them, 'What are you having for lunch?' and then made the foods they craved."

Soon, the word spread, and the line at lunch would be out the door. Chairs that hung on the walls would be taken down and added to a table to make room for more diners. It wasn't uncommon for strangers to share a table, which made for a lively atmosphere, another trait that still lingers at Café Poca Cosa.

If you got there late, say, after 2:00 p.m., you were out of luck. Davila closed promptly at that time, no exceptions. That's when she had to leave to pick up her kids at school.

Davila and her sister would often drive to Mexico to purchase the ingredients, which, in the early days, weren't readily available in Tucson.

They'd tow a trailer and then fill it with chiles and spices and whatever looked delicious.

One daily visitor, a Mr. Lopez, was the manager of the Santa Rita Hotel, which was located a half block south. He pestered Davila to take over the kitchen at the hotel. "We were happy," she said. "We were working with a little stove. We had six tables. We didn't need more. It was perfect." Still, she checked out the site. "The kitchen at the hotel was so big you could roller skate in it," she said.

But Davila has a way about her, a philosophy that she lives by: "If you don't jump into the fire and figure it out," you'll never know what could have been.

Realizing the move didn't mean she couldn't keep both places open, she enlisted her sisters to help. Marcella lived in Tucson, but Sandra was living in Florida, where she ran her own restaurant. Davila knew that her sister missed the family, so she persuaded Sandra to move back to Tucson and share managing duties with Marcella at the smaller restaurant, which was soon renamed Poca Cosa Cosa.

"Our family is very tight," said Davila.

The hotel dining room was transformed into a bright, colorful riot of colors. Purples, reds, greens and yellows covered the walls. Mexican milagros, religious icons, rustic paintings and loud tunes added to the whole experience. The menu was presented to tables on a chalkboard, and servers would explain each dish in detail. The go-to favorite became the Plato Poca Cosa, in which diners put their trust in the chef, who would use three entrées to create a dish designed for each diner. A huge salad, charro beans and warm flour tortillas accompanied every meal.

With the move, dinner was added and people came in droves. But it wasn't just the locals who discovered Davila's dishes. Soon, the national press was singing the praises of Café Poca Cosa. An article by Jane and Michael Stern appeared in *Gourmet* magazine, and others followed, including *Men's Journal*, *Bon Appetit*, *Better Homes and Gardens*, *Wine Spectator* and the *New York Times*. Poca Cosa wasn't so little anymore.

In 2005, the Santa Rita Hotel was converted into apartments, and Poca Cosa had to move. Davila opted for a new space housed under a recently built parking garage. Decor changed dramatically. Davila went modern and sleek, with small touches from the old space. People flipped out, certain that this meant the end of the Poca Cosa they loved. But there was nothing to worry about. Davila's commitment to great food and fine service remained.

Davila is known as a stern boss, but she's not past washing windows or sweeping floors. She herself is an example of hard work that has resulted in many loyal employees. "We have people working with us for a long time, twenty, twenty-five years," Davila said. "That's unheard of."

Meanwhile, back at the "Little One," big changes were happening. The tiny building was located just steps from the federal courthouse and, until 9/11, being neighbors had never been a problem. But the feds decided that the restaurant posed a threat and demanded it be torn down. Losing the building was heartbreaking, but with typical Davila pluck, the sisters moved their restaurant to the busy corner of Stone Avenue and Pennington Street without missing a beat.

The Davilas are also big on giving back. They've built schools and churches in Mexico. At the "Little One," a big jar rests on the counter for donations to help buy shoes and clothing for poor families in Mexico.

Today, Poca Cosa remains a destination restaurant. People from all over the United States, even the world, come to taste Davila's creations. Davila's daughter Shanali is the pastry chef. Her son Christopher runs the front of the house and tends bar. And on any given night, when she isn't in the kitchen, Davila can be found greeting her guests—her "family."

## New Delhi Palace / Cuisine of India (1987)
### From an Interview with Yatin and Naval Parekh

There were several owners of the New Delhi Palace before Yatin and Naval Parekh purchased this eastside restaurant in 2006, one being Naval's brother. And while the restaurant made claim as the first Indian restaurant in Tucson, it was under the guidance of the Parekhs that New Delhi Palace became a favorite place to enjoy the cuisine of India.

Yatin was an IT guy and had been transferred to Tucson from his company in New Delhi. Naval began helping out her brother at the restaurant. In India, she had a culinary background, so when the restaurant was put on the market, the Parekhs bought the place. In 2007, Yatin retired from his job to devote himself to the restaurant. Naval noted that his tech background plays a big part in their success.

The Parekhs altered the basic layout, including moving the storeroom and a bathroom to make movement more practical, relocating the bar to the front room, installing a permanent buffet table and upgrading parts of the kitchen.

But it was their attention to "Truthfulness" that made a difference in how people in Tucson would learn about authentic Indian food. Yatin explained the definition of truthfulness: "I mean, not cutting corners, buying the freshest of ingredients, operating it like a family." Today, they source all herbs, spices, lentils, flours, rice and more from India. Every dish is made fresh as the ticket comes into the kitchen, including all sauces, which are often made ahead of time in other restaurants. "There are no shortcuts. We don't do that here," said Naval. Even the yogurt is made in-house.

The softly lit dining room is beautifully decorated. Airbrushed murals depict various scenes of India. Tablecloths are topped with lacy runners and tiny trinkets imported from India. Indian music plays softly in the background. Customers appreciate the quiet, elegant ambiance.

Presentation is artistic. Entrées are served in large copper pots called kahrai. The Peshawari lamb chops arrive in a tiny metal bucket. Attention to detail extends even to the basmati rice, which is presented in stylish urns. Cocktails are Indian influenced. House-blended teas and lassis are numerous and eclectic. All of these elements make New Delhi Palace stand out from the many other Indian restaurants that have come and gone.

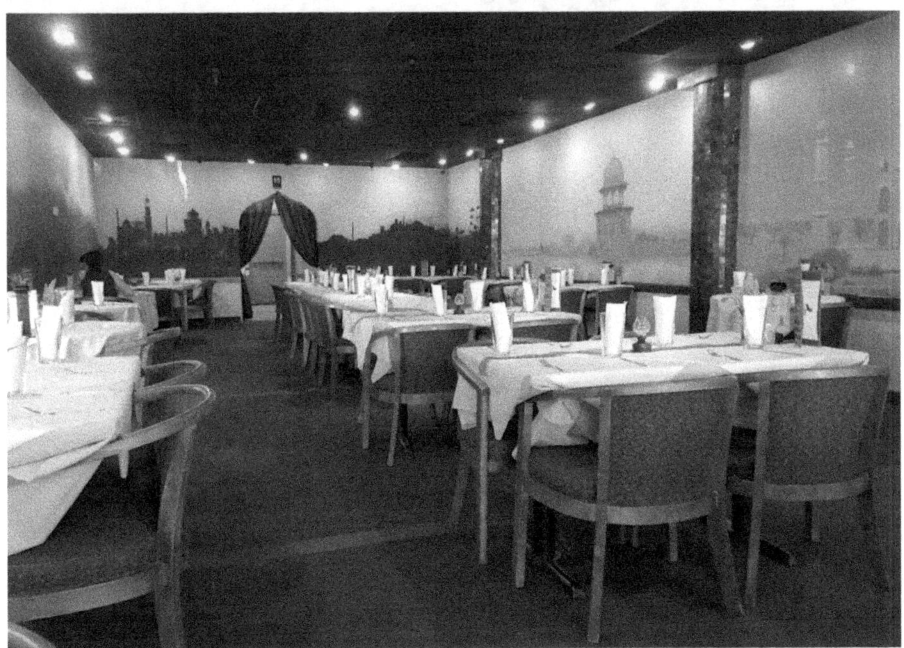

New Delhi Palace is known as one of those restaurants where diners can enjoy a quiet dinner with friends. *Author photo.*

The Parekhs also practice the ancient science of Ayurveda. Ayurveda dates back thousands of years, as far back as the Indus Valley. In the simplest terms, Ayurveda is a holistic approach to achieving balance in life. The Parekhs bring the concept to all aspects of New Delhi Palace.

Tea blends all contribute to greater health and well-being. They are so popular that snowbirds call Yatin, asking him to ship them the blends.

Truthfulness is also a part of the front of the house. Servers are trained to engage the diners in their preferences regarding certain dishes and the levels of heat. Either Yatin or Naval visits every table to get feedback, and if the response isn't excellent, they ask what could have been done differently. They listen and do what is necessary to make the customers happy.

The menu is expansive. Naval noted that each state in India has its own customs, flavors, ingredients and preparation techniques. "There is so much more to Indian food than north and south," said Naval. "We've covered all twenty-eight states of India. We're constantly learning. The customers have embraced this." The Parekhs point out that palates in India are vastly different than those in America. While Americans taste the complex flavors of the spices, native Indians palates are more about the heat. Food found in India tends to have an oilier texture.

As the world has gotten smaller, customers are more accustomed to the foods, flavors and cultures of India. Yatin said that back when the Parekhs opened the restaurant, customers were surprised the two of them spoke English, and some even asked if elephants roamed the streets of New Delhi.

All of that has changed. Today, customers are more knowledgeable about the wonders of India, yet Yatin and Naval still love to teach guests about their country and their food. Dining at New Delhi Palace continues to nourish both mind and body.

# 1990s

## *Population: Tucson, 405,390; Pima County, 666,880*

As the twentieth century came to an end, folks in Tucson were as busy as ever. Construction continued at a rapid pace. Copper mining was going strong. People moved to the area in great numbers.

News from Tucson included everything from a glass-enclosed experiment in sustainable living to a massive fire at a major tourist attraction to a national championship and a gold medal athlete.

In September 1991, eight people entered a massive glass structure in Oracle, about a thirty-minute drive north of Tucson. Biosphere 2 was a gigantic experiment in sustainable living. The structure was 3.14 acres in size and enclosed in glass, divided into three ecosystems. Eight people—four men and four women—planned to grow all of their own food, recycle their waste and conduct experiments, all for the betterment of the planet. But things went sour quickly. Among health issues, air quality and infighting, Biosphere 2 was in trouble. Local press had a field day with all the hassles. Participants lasted the two years, but their efforts were considered by many locals to be a failure. These days, Biosphere 2 is operated by UA with the mission of advancing an understanding of both natural and man-made issues. Tours are available daily.

On April 24, 1994, just as tourists were leaving Old Tucson after a show, crews discovered a fire in the sign shop. Early attempts to extinguish the fire failed due to a hose that wasn't long enough and a lack of water pressure. As the fire spread through the old wooden structures, local fire departments arrived. Everyone pitched in to prevent the fire from spreading. In the end, 70 percent of the structures were lost, along with irreplaceable memorabilia from movies and television shows. Arson was the cause. Even though a person confessed to the crime, the case is still open. Old Tucson reopened in January 1997.

On a lighter note, for Wildcat fans, dreams came true when UA's men's basketball team, with Lute Olsen at the helm, beat three number one–seeded teams to win the national championship. Kerri Strug, a local teenager, was part of the Olympic gold medal women's gymnastics team. Concerts included Garth Brooks, ZZ Top and Fleetwood Mac, who performed the only concert ever held at UA's football stadium.

A change on the restaurant scene had a major impact, when owners formed the Tucson Originals. The group's mission was to promote Tucson's restaurants, especially since so many chains were opening all over the city. The restaurants opening in this decade reflected the changes in dining found elsewhere in the United States. Chefs who had worked at many of the best restaurants in Tucson were opening their own places. Wine lists expanded to include more than just "whites," "reds" and "rosés." Tucsonans were becoming foodies.

## THE CUP CAFÉ (1990)
### FROM A PHONE INTERVIEW WITH RICHARD AND SHANA OSERAN

Located off the lobby in the historic Hotel Congress, the Cup has been a favorite of Tucson diners since opening in 1990.

But that was long before downtown Tucson became the hip place to go for dining and drinking. Richard and Shana Oseran bought the hotel in 1985, when nobody went downtown. They inherited about a dozen permanent residents, a tired bar and a barely there restaurant space.

With their keen eye for style and detail, they turned the hotel into a happening place, adding a nightclub, Club Congress, which became a popular music venue garnering national attention. The Tap Room, a bar that has been in the hotel since forever, was dressed up a little and became the place to be. The lobby was turned into a work of art, with details painted by Larry Boyce. Rooms are now rented to tourists. The Oserans maintained the history of the hotel. The old switchboard is used as it was back in the day, and people can use phone booths that sit in the lobby, although a call costs more than a nickel.

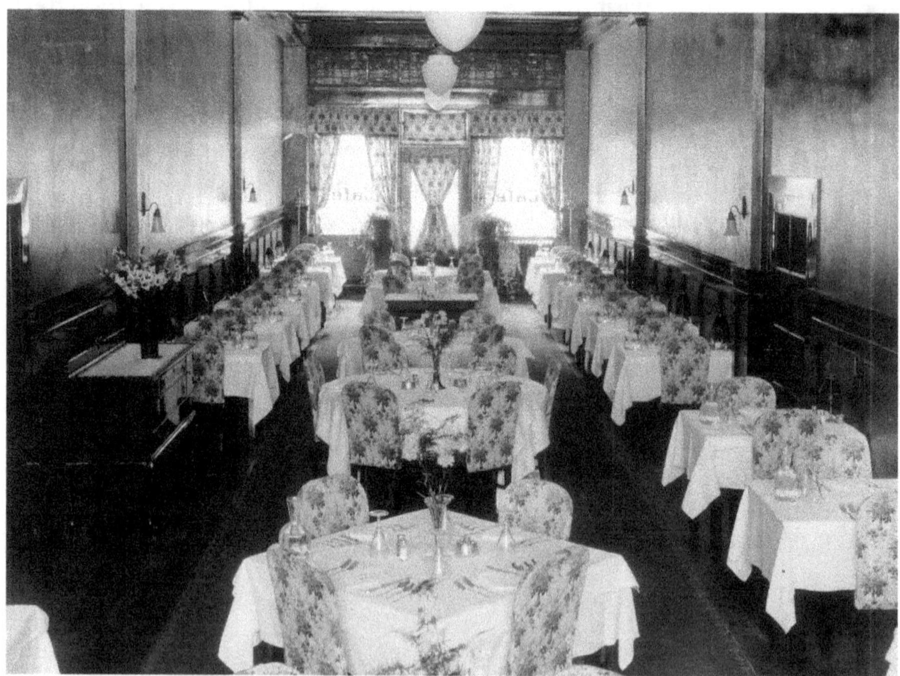

An early photo from the café at Hotel Congress. *Courtesy Richard and Shana Oseran, Hotel Congress.*

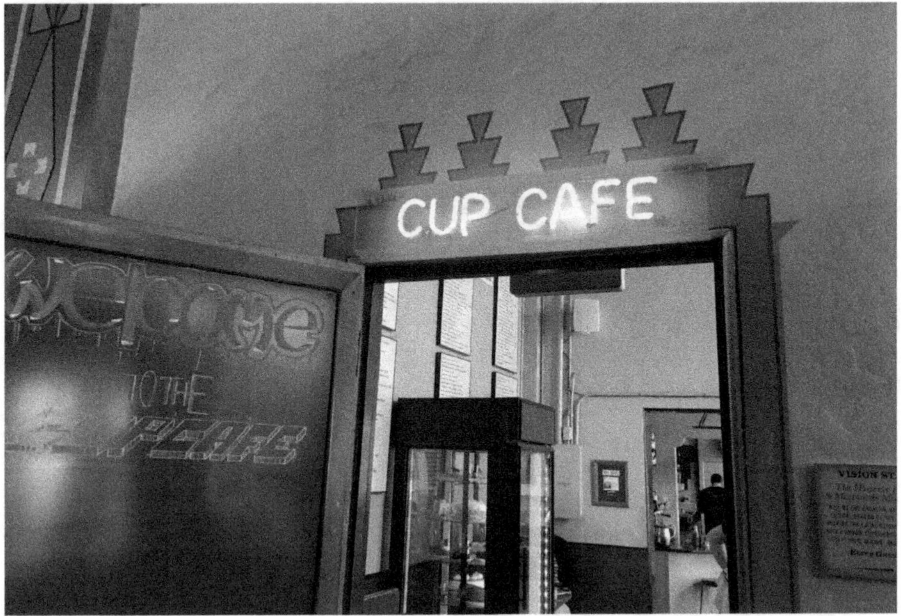


The Cup Café in the Hotel Congress serves three meals a day and delicious cocktails. *Author photo.*

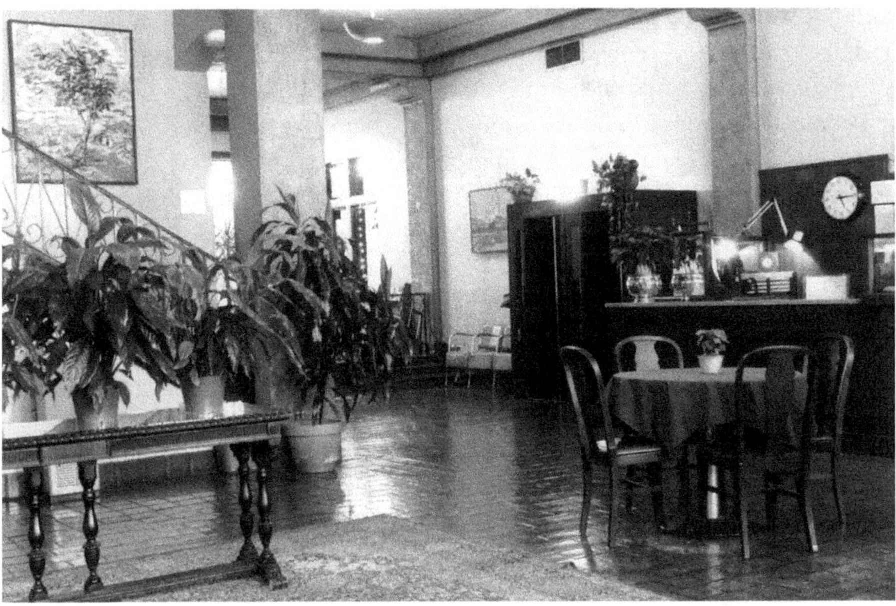

The phone booths and front desk are still standing in the lobby at Hotel Congress. *Courtesy Richard and Shana Oseran, Hotel Congress.*

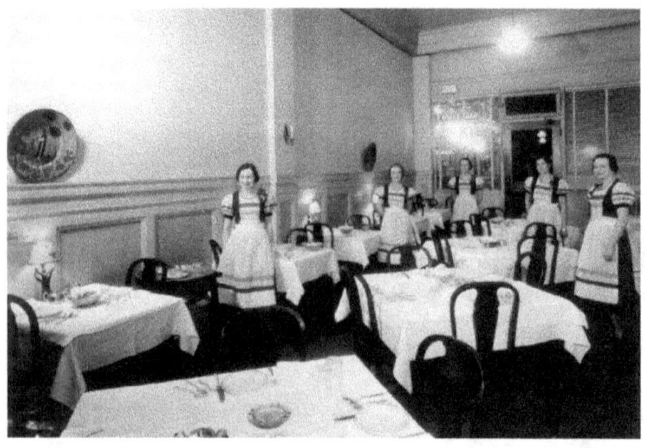

Servers at the ready at the original café at the Hotel Congress. *Courtesy Richard and Shana Oseran, Hotel Congress.*

The restaurant was first operated by a young couple and called Bowen & Bailey. When they bowed out, the Oserans took over, renaming it the Cup.

Looking at the space today, it's hard to imagine what those early days were like. Food choices and seating were limited, because the only cooking element was a hot plate and there was only one tiny room. But little by little, the Oserans made improvements to the Cup. They added a room, built a new and more accessible kitchen, added a bar/counter and extended the patio. Some improvements were major, like installing air conditioning; other changes were more cosmetic, like the penny floor. Inspired by a table they had re-covered in pennies, the Oserans and employees tiled the floor with 177,000 pennies, a one-of-a-kind project and highly durable.

People feel strongly about traditions at the Cup. Years ago, in order to make room for some poetry readings, Shana temporarily took down a large poster that was filled with quirky truisms. The uproar was so loud, even the newspaper got involved.

The menu went through some changes over time. In 2000, the Cup went continental and hired a French chef. The menu was short-lived. Breakfast, lunch and dinner are served daily. Today's menu is more eclectic, with hints of the Southwest and a long list of favorite dishes at breakfast, lunch and dinner. Desserts, which are displayed in the sparkling case in the front room, are still the recipes of Baker Bill, who, after decades of baking, moved into a bookkeeping position. Servers and kitchen staff also have racked up years at the Cup. In 2003, Rachel Ray from the Food Network featured the Railroad Breakfast on her *$40 a Day* program.

Home to many annual festivals, Hotel Congress celebrates Dillinger Days with the reenactment of the capture of John Dillinger, Public Enemy No. 1, who stayed at the hotel in 1934.

Unlike most diners, alcohol is available, and people can build their own Bloody Marys.

The Cup is the grand dame of downtown dining, but dining here continues to be a hip event, no matter the time of day.

## Sakura (1991)

Known as "Mr. An," Kwan C An has one of the most recognizable faces in Tucson. The other is Lute Olsen. Olsen earned fame by taking the UA basketball team to multiple championships. An became famous for the various restaurants and for television ads in which he is the star.

Sakura was not An's first restaurant, nor was it the first Japanese restaurant in Tucson, but both An and Sakura elevated the experiences of teppan dining, sushi and sake.

An was born in Korea in 1940 and took a long, hard and circuitous route to Tucson and to the restaurant industry. But he had the touch, and each restaurant he opened became highly successful.

Sakura opened in 1991 on the far east side. A second one, on the northwest side, opened in 2001. During that time, An became as well known for his face as for his food and his extensive philanthropy. He sold the second Sakura to Benihana in 2005 and the original in 2008 to a group from Phoenix.

The original Sakura is still going strong, and An, despite having retired once or twice, now runs Mr. An's at the site of the former northwest Sakura.

## El Guero Canelo (1993)

Daniel Contrares, El Guero Canelo himself, may not have been the originator of the Sonoran hot dog, but he certainly took this tasty concoction to another level. Contrares started with a food cart and then moved his operations to a rehabbed drive-in on South Twelfth Avenue.

The super casual restaurant became so popular, people waited for tables like they do in fancy restaurants in big cities. The crowds are a mix of neighbors, government workers, fire and police personnel, teenagers and families—in other words, everyone. Mariachi music blares above. The whole atmosphere is straight out of Mexico. You order at the window and then watch your lunch being made at an outdoor grill. The dogs are wrapped in bacon and then topped with pinto beans, salsa, chopped tomatoes, mayo,

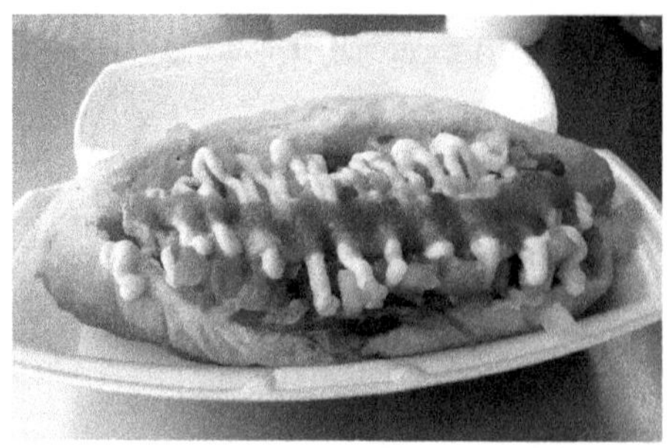

There's nothing like a Sonoran hot dog. *festivefood@wordpress.com posted by reilly8.*

mustard and both grilled and raw onions and served on a soft bun made especially for these dogs. The dogs have been featured on multiple shows on the Food Channel, in *USA Today*, on NBC News and more. A second El Guero was built on the north side of town several years later, but the original restaurant is where it's at.

## KINGFISHER (1993)

One of the greatest compliments a restaurant can get is when other restaurant people eat there. Kingfisher is just such an establishment. In interviews, when local chefs are asked to name their favorite restaurants, Kingfisher comes up again and again. But the midtown restaurant is also popular with the regular diners, as evidenced by being named the best seafood restaurant in all major Tucson publications.

Jim "Murph" Murphy, Jeff Azersky, Tim Ivankovich and John Burke had worked together in various combinations at other places in Tucson. So, when they opened Kingfisher in 1993, they had a built-in crowd, but they also attracted a larger audience who loved the casual atmosphere and the delicious American fare.

Murph had learned the ropes of seafood at Jerome's, and Azersky was a transplant from the South Shore of Massachusetts, so there was plenty of knowledge and experience in that area. Ivankovich and Burke had years of experience in the front of the house. But the team knew they needed more than just great seafood.

Marianne Banes was the perfect choice. Banes had a stellar culinary résumé and was hired to create desserts. Kingfisher introduced Tucson's first late-night menu. They lightened up the dining room. (In its previous incarnation, the building had been home to the Iron Mask, which had the look of an old English tavern.) The bar, though, retained much of the same look, including the original Iron Mask bar chairs. Murph talked about how, when they moved a heavy refrigerator from the kitchen to behind the bar, all went well until they had to lift the item over the bar. Somehow, the mission was accomplished, but it hasn't been moved since.

In 1999, Burke left to open Fiorito's, an Italian eatery nearby, but the friends continued. In 2005, they opened Bluefin Seafood Bistro on the northwest side. That restaurant closed in 2015.

In 2012, Ivankovich died unexpectedly at the age of fifty-four. The team felt the loss deeply, but they moved forward, always with their friend in mind. Aided by a team that has been with them for years, Murph and Azersky take turns in the kitchen and in the front of the house. On any given night, the dining room is filled to capacity and people stand three-deep at the bar.

The regular menu always contains a choice of oysters from every coast and other fresh seafood options. Annual festivities include an Oysterfest, Fat Tuesday celebration and a summer-long Road Trip around America.

Murph credits the longevity to attention to detail. Tucsonans credit the longevity to a fine place to relax over great seafood, a couple of cocktails or a glass of wine from the American-centric wine list.

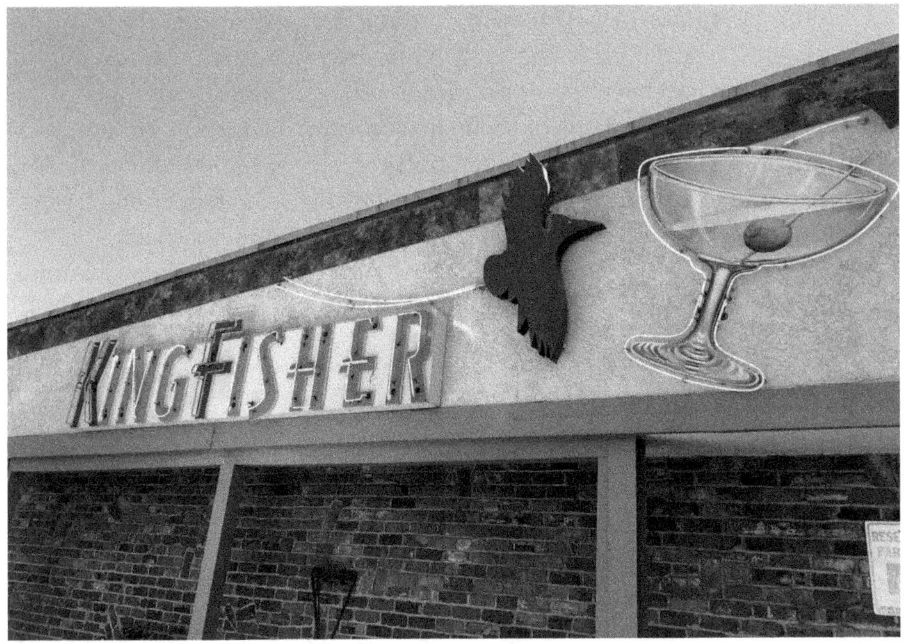


Kingfisher brought the ocean to Tucson. *Author photo.*

## VIVACE (1993)

Vivace has deep roots. Owner-chef Daniel Scordato's family owned and operated Scordato's from 1972 through the early 1980s, and Danny ran the highly successful Daniel's for several years.

Scordato's was white-tablecloth Italian dining, and Danny worked there from the time he was fifteen years old. So, when he opened Vivace in a midtown upscale (at least at the time) shopping plaza, the place was packed every night. Diners could enjoy many of the old Scordato standards, as well as new dishes created by Danny.

In 2001, Vivace moved to new digs in St. Philip's Plaza. This location was much closer to the monied foothills neighborhoods and attracted a whole new crowd. There was a built-in oven, an Italian-laden wine list and a patio that would win awards from several local publications. The menu featured a mix of pastas, grilled meats and seafood dishes straight out of an Italian seaside village.

Decor was very Italian as well. Colorful tiles, dark wood, tiled floors, huge vases filled with fresh flowers and smooth, well-trained service meant a memorable evening no matter the occasion.

In 2009, Scordato opened Vivace Pizzeria across the plaza. In 2014, in what can only be called moving on up, Scordato relocated to a building in the foothills that had been the home of two other previous restaurants.

The site was located on one of the highest commercial lots in Tucson, with amazing views of mountains at lunch and the city at night. The cathedral ceilings and huge picture windows made everything seem bigger and bolder. The decor was still Italian but definitely more urban and polished.

Vivace continues to be popular. During high season—basically mid-November to late March—diners often need to make reservations weeks in advance.

## PASTICHE (1997)

On a sunny February afternoon in 2017, the parking lot at Pastiche was packed. The reason wasn't one of the charity events Pastiche was known for, nor was there a wine tasting, another hallmark of this popular restaurant.

Hundreds of people gathered to say goodbye to their friend, their mentor and their boss—Pat Connors.

Connors had been diagnosed with lung cancer the previous October and decided he wanted to take charge of the end of his life, so he and his wife, Julie, invited the community to share stories, eat great food made by other restaurateurs, listen to music and give Pat a hug or two. He called it a "living wake." The line wrapped around the restaurant for hours, but no one minded, nor was anyone surprised. It seemed every restaurant owner, chef, food writer, bartender, wine representative and customer who had ever eaten at Pastiche was there. Everyone wanted to say goodbye, but they also wanted to say thank-you for all Pat had done through the years. Pat had been a huge part of the Tucson restaurant scene even before he and Julie opened Pastiche in March 1998.

Pastiche was all about American food kicked up a notch or two, and Tucsonans loved it. Food was cleverly prepared. Wine was plentiful and reasonably priced. "You want people to enjoy it, don't you?" Pat told me years before. There were great cocktails. And the vibe was warm and casual.

Pat and Julie, charter members of the Tucson Originals, were involved in promoting Local Arizona. The Connorses were also known and admired for their years of philanthropy in Tucson. They actively participated in the Primavera Cooks fundraiser, in which people could work in the kitchen side by side with chefs. Primavera Foundation is a local organization whose mission is to help people out of poverty. Dine Out for Safety, the Bald Beauty Project and many more charities benefited from Pat and Julie's kindness, hard work and passion.

Pat died less than a week after the wake, and the restaurant was sold three weeks later.

The new owners hope to carry on the great service, food and bar programs the Connorses started twenty years ago.

6

# Let's See What Tomorrow Brings

If the numbers are any indication, the future of Tucson dining looks rosy. Almost 63 percent of food-related businesses are locally owned, compared to the national average of 41 percent. Locally owned means that seventy-three cents of every dollar spent stays in the community. The nation's hospitality industry supports twenty-four thousand jobs, and tourism generated $52.8 billion in 2015.

New restaurants featuring southern comfort food, Vietnamese, Korean, sushi, poke bowls, barbecue, all-American fare and even modern takes on Mexican can be found all over town. The number of food trucks rose by 12 percent, while several established food trucks have moved into brick-and-mortar places.

Where once it was difficult to find a farmers' market, now there are twenty different markets on different days of the week, and the number of people creating artisanal food products found at those markets has increased 25 percent. Craft breweries have grown by 42 percent, and distilleries have doubled (from one to two, but that is an increase).

The City of Gastronomy designation made a huge impact. In 2016, the story translated into $15.5 million of free media coverage, compared to the previous year of around $5.5 million. The *New York Times*, *USA Today*, *Food & Wine*, *National Geographic* and *Smithsonian* ran feature stories.

But can all these elements be sustained? Yes, they can, because of the strength of connections in the culinary community and because Tucsonans are big on "Keeping It Local." People in Tucson also have enormous appetites for the new and the old.

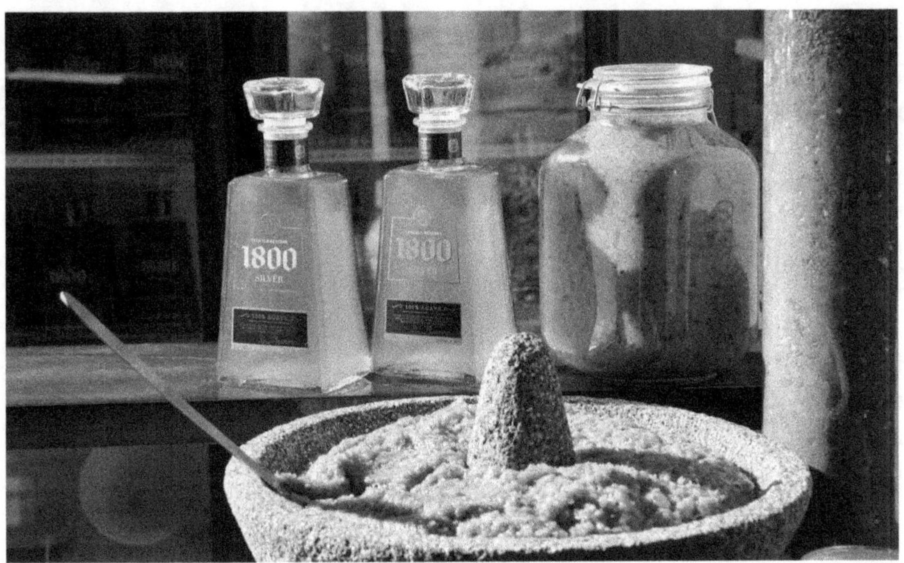


Southern Arizona Arts & Culture Alliance's Tequila and Salsa Festival is a fun and charitable event. *Courtesy SAACA.*

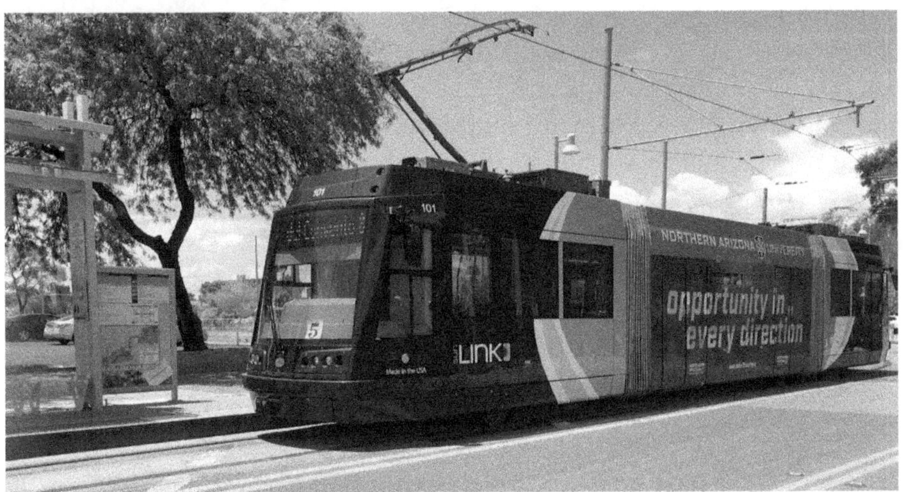


Take a ride on the Modern Street Car. *Author photo.*

As varied as the restaurants in this book are, they do have several traits in common. This was apparent when talking to the owners and employees. One question I always asked was, "Why do you think you have remained so popular?" Inevitably, three phrases came up. The first was "consistent." While Ralph Waldo Emerson noted "a foolish consistency is the hobgoblin of little minds," here, the consistency is wise and offers diners a certain reliability and comfort in both food and service. Customers can come in any day of the week and order their favorite dish and know they will get the same flavors, the same portion and, most important, the same great service.

The second answer was "good employees." The owners understood the differences good employees make in the day-to-day workings of a restaurant and appreciated the loyalty and hard work. In some cases, people retired from places at which they started when they were young. Others worked their way up and became active participants in the businesses, even owners. A few left for an assortment of reasons but then returned to a place they considered home and people they considered family.

The third concept, and perhaps the most important, was "hospitality." Every person I talked with mentioned how much they valued their customers, wanting to make them happy.

Several other topics were on the minds of the owners. In 2016, the State of Arizona enacted a plan to raise the minimum wage to $12.00 over a period of four years. The new law also required employers to grant an hour of sick leave for every thirty hours worked. Then, in the spring of 2017, the voters of Tucson approved a $0.05 sales tax increase for road improvements and police and fire department equipment. The tax will expire in five years.

All owners understood the need for such measures but were concerned about how the added costs would affect their bottom line. Only time will tell.

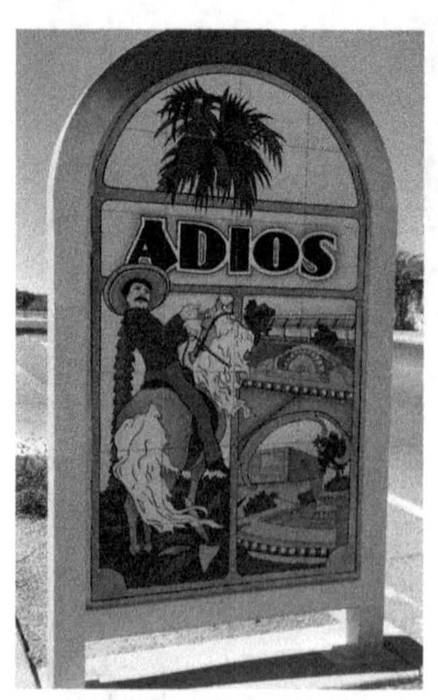

Adios. *Author photo.*

Almost everyone mentioned the importance of adapting to the needs and tastes of customers. In this respect, menus across the board have more vegetarian, vegan and gluten-free options.

No mention was made of another common theme. The culinary community loves to give back. Every year, hundreds of charities benefit from the generosity of the restaurants in this book; it would be impossible to list them all.

Therefore, utilizing the information gathered for this book, we can honestly say that the Tucson restaurant scene is healthy, happy and hopeful for the future.

# Bibliography

## *Books and Articles*


Allis, Brad. "Historic Marana Steakhouse Has a Rich History." *Inside Tucson Business*, July 22, 2016.

———. "Restaurant Linked with Davis-Monthan Since 1956." *Tucson Business*, October 16, 2015.

Altimirano, Mari. "Pat's Chili Dogs: Good Enough to Die For." *Tucson Citizen*, August 24, 1995.

*Arizona Daily Star*. "Carry-out Café Planned." September 3, 1961.

Auslander, Edith Sayre. "Mexican Food Row." *Arizona Daily Star,* October 30, 1977.

Barker, Scott. "All American…and More." *Tucson Lifestyle*, May 2017.

Boran, Rebecca. "He Found His Niche." *Arizona Daily Star*, April 20, 2008.

Burba Trulson, Nora. "Rincon Market. 50 of Our Favorite Places to Eat at in Arizona." *Arizona Highways* (2011).

Burch, Cathalena E. "Lil' Abner's Put on the Market." *Arizona Daily Star*, June 19, 2015.

———. "Molina's Midway Mexican Food: A 64-year Affair." *Arizona Daily Star*, May 15. 2017.

———. "Tucson Builder to Re-open Saguaro Corners." *Arizona Daily Star*, February 15, 2013.

———. "Tucson's Celebrity Restaurateur Sells Sakura." *Arizona Daily Star*, July 26, 2008.

Carmody, Neil, ed. *Whiskey, Six-Guns and Red Light Ladies: George Hand's Saloon Diaries 1875–1878*. Silver City, NM: High-Lonesome Books, 1995.

Chesnick, Mike. "Hillenbrand Left His Mark on UA Stadium." Obituary. *Tucson Citizen*, March 18, 2003.

Clinco, Demion. "The DeGrazia Fabrics, a Collusion of Western Art and Fashion." Tucson Modernism Week 2015. Arizona Lithographers, Tucson, Arizona.

———. *Historic Miracle Mile Tucson's Northern Auto Gateway: A Historic Context Study for the Oracle Area.* Prepared for the City of Tucson's Historic Preservation Office, Department of Urban Planning and Design, 2009.

Connelly, Rita. "A Chinese Constant." *Tucson Weekly*, March 17, 2011.

———. "Indie Inspirations." *Tucson Weekly*, February 9, 2006.

———. "In the Kitchen." *Tucson Weekly*, March 18, 2010.

Cooper, Abraham. "The Legend of El Tiradito." *Zocolo* (May 2011).

Copenhaven, Larry. "Lil' Abner's Serves Thousands of Steaks Every Week." *Tucson Citizen*, February 9, 1999.

Davis-Monthan Air Force Base. "History." June 2, 2009. http://www.dm.af.mil.

Delgado, Grace Pena. "Of Kith and Kin: Land, Leases and Guanxi in Tucson's Chinese and Mexican Communities 1880s–1920s." *Journal of Arizona History* (Spring 2005). Published by the Arizona Historical Society.

*Developing Marshall Square: Developing the West University Community*. http://www.parentseyes.edu.

Devine, Dave. "Twenty Years Later." *Tucson Weekly*, September 25, 2003.

Downing, Renee. "The Blue Willow Special." *Tucson Weekly*, July 27, 2006.

Duarte, Carmen. "Casa Molina, Sister's Cooking Blazed New Frontier." *Arizona Daily Star*, April 30, 1981.

Duffy, Ruth, Linda Lowe, John V. Long and John Foltz. *Menus of Tucson's Finest Restaurants*. Paradise Valley, AZ: Quail Run Publications, 1978.

*Entertainment Magazine*. "Tucson's Culture of Fried Chicken: The Polar Bar" 1 (2014).

Flores, Carlotta. *El Charro Café: The Tastes & Traditions of Tucson*. Tucson, AZ: Fisher Books, 1998.

Fong, Lawrence Michael. "Sojourners and Settlers: The Chinese Experience in Arizona." *Journal of Arizona History* 1 (Autumn 1980).

Fourthavenue.org.

Gasper, John. "Neither Cowboys nor Gourmets Will Go Hungry." *Chicago Tribune*, March 29, 1987.

Hansen, Greg. "Hillenbrand 'Just a Down to Earth Guy'—Philanthropist Aided U of A's Growth." *Arizona Daily Star*, June 26, 1994.

Hansen, Ronald J. "Tucson Misses Spring Training; Chandler Has No Regrets." *Arizona Republic*, March 25, 2014.

Happe, Marguerite. "Dishing Up History." *Tucson Lifestyle* (Winter/Spring 2016/2017).

Henry, Bonnie. "Club 21, Family Roots." *Arizona Daily Star*, January 8, 2009.

Itole, Bruce. "El Corral. 50 of Our Favorite Places to Eat at in Arizona." *Arizona Highways* (2011).

Jarolim, Edie. "A Food and a Family Force." *BizTucson*, February 26, 2015.

Kemar Rei, Pradeep. "Tucson Post World War II Residential Subdivision Development." Akros, Inc. Wilson Preservation, Coffman Studios. LLX HDC. 2007.

Kimble, Megan. "A Gastronomy of Place: Reimaging Baja Arizona's Future by Peering into Its Past." *Edible Baja Arizona* 1 (January-February 2015).

———. "Our City of Gastronomy." *Edible Baja Arizona* 15 (November-December 2015).

Kimmelman, Alex Jay. "Luring Tourists to Tucson: Civic Promotion During the 1920s." *Journal of Arizona History* 28, no. 2 (Summer 1981): 135–54.

Kjos, Tiffany. "George Miller, Tucson Mayor in 1990s, Dies." *Arizona Daily Star*, December 25, 2014.

Mabry, Dr. Jonathan. Data collected from Visit Tucson, City of Tucson, U.S. Census. University of Arizona Economic & Business Research Center, Pima County Health Department.

Matis, Kimberly. "Frank Calvert: Saguaro Corners Restaurant Was Where He Loved to Be." *Arizona Daily Star*, August 7, 2007.

———. "Gus Balon: He Never Gussies Up Balon's Home-style Fare." *Arizona Daily Star*, March 20, 2007.

———. "Saguaro Corners Turns Golden." *Arizona Daily Star*, February, 23, 2005.

Myal, Susan. *Mexican Restaurants: Recipes, Repasts and Remembrances*. Tucson: University of Arizona Press, 1999.

North-Hager, Eddie. "Pat's Founder Made Signature Chili." *Tucson Citizen*, March 4, 1999.

Old Tucson. "Film History." http://oldtucson.com/films-producers-directors/film-history.

Oliverz-Giles, Nathan. "Pat's Chili Dogs: Barrio Classic, City Icon." *El Independente*, October 2006.

Paganelli Votto, Mary. *Food Lovers' Guide to Tucson*. Guilford, CT: Morris Book Publishing, 2013.

Persa, H.G., John T. Self, David Njita and Tiffany King. "Why Restaurants Fail." *Cornell Hotel and Restaurant Administration Quarterly* 48, no. 3 (August 2005).

Pierce, H. Wesley, and Peter L. Kresen. "The Floods of October 1983." *Fieldnotes, Arizona Bureau of Geology & Mineral Technology* 14, no. 2 (Summer 1984).

Regan, Margaret. "The Chapters of El Charro." *Edible Baja Arizona* (January/February 2017).

———. "There Goes the Neighborhood." *Tucson Weekly*, March 12, 1997.

Ring, Bob, and Al Ring. "Tucson's Unprecedented Growth 1950's–1970's." Tucsonfirefoundation.com.

Rogers, W. Lane. "Dillinger Arrested in Tucson." *Arizona Capitol Times*, January 4, 2011.

Russell, Matt. "Tucson's Raw Bar Culture." *Inside Tucson Business*, October 31, 2014.
Sonnichsen, C.L. *Tucson: The Life and Times of an American City*. Norman: University of Oklahoma Press, 1987.
Stauffer, Tom. "81-Year-Old Rincon Market to Be Sold." *Arizona Daily Star*, January 23, 2008.
Stern, Jane, and Michael Stern. *Blue Plate Specials & Blue Ribbon Cafes*. New York: Lebhan-Friedman Books, 2001.
———. "Café Poca Cosa." Roadfood.com.
———. "Gus Balon's." Roadfood.com.
———. "Pat's Drive In." Roadfood.com.
*Tucson Cooks! An Extraordinary Culinary Adventure*. Tucson, AZ: Primavera Foundation, 2005.
*Tucson: Official City and County Magazine* 2, no. 8 (August 1929).
University of Arizona. "UA History and Traditions." http://www.arizona.edu/topics/about-university/about-university-arizona/ua-history-and-traditions.
Vinyard, Valerie. "Mi Nidito Celebrates 65 Years in Business." *BizTucson* (Summer 2017).
War, Coley. "Mr. On the Move." *Arizona Daily Star*, June 10, 2010.
Yancy, James Walter. "The Negro in Tucson; Past and Present." Master's thesis, University of Arizona, 1933.

## *Websites*

Athenson4thAvenue.com.
Bluewillow.com.
CasaMolina.com.
Codysbeefnbeans.com.
Cushingstreet.com.
Elcharrocafe.com.
Elminuto.com.
Laindita.net.
Luckywishbone.com.
Minidito.net.
Molinasmidway.com.
Tucsonaz.gov.
Tucson.com.
Tucsonfirefightersfoundation.com.
TucsonMuseum.org.
Tucsonweekly.com.

# *Index*

## E



## F



## G



## H



## I



## J



## K



## L



## M

**N**



**O**



**P**



**R**



**S**



**T**



**U**



**W**



**Y**



**Z**

# About the Author

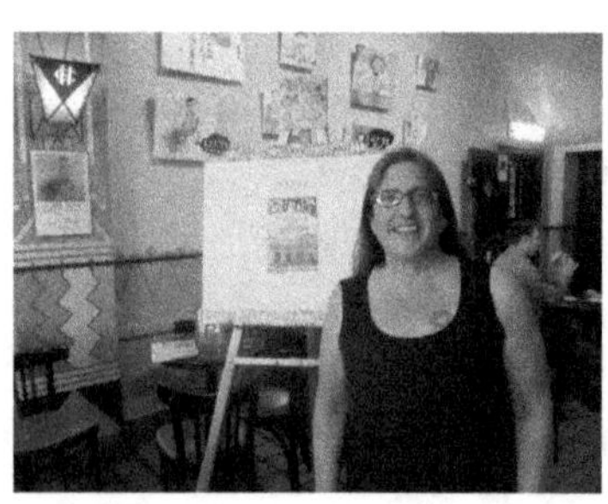

Rita Connelly has lived and dined in Tucson since 1972. She moved back to her Wisconsin roots for a while but then came to her senses after a couple of cold, cold winters.

Her first published piece covered insurance claims; she switched to food writing shortly thereafter. She was the restaurant reviewer for the *Tucson Weekly* for ten years and was the Tucson contributing writer for gayot.com. During that time, she developed both professional and personal relationships with cooks, servers, restaurant owners, diners, food writers, media personnel and more, all of whom helped contribute to this book.

Her other work includes *Lost Restaurants of Tucson* (The History Press) and *Insider's Guide to Tucson*, as well as articles in Visit Tucson, Experiencing Sedona, Highroads, sallysplace.com and other local and national publications. Her blog, wellfedfoodieblog.wordpress.com, covers all that's happening on the Tucson culinary scene. She has a Facebook page of the same name.

She lives with her husband, John, just minutes from many of the restaurants found in this book. Her next book is all about Arizona's chimichangas and will be published by The History Press sometime in 2018.

www.ingramcontent.com/pod-product-compliance
Lightning Source LLC
LaVergne TN
LVHW010939100826
845153LV00001B/87
* 9 7 8 1 5 4 0 2 2 8 1 8 5 *